6/16

# MAO ZEDONG
## AND THE
# CHINESE
# REVOLUTION

### Ann Malaspina

**Enslow Publishing**
101 W. 23rd Street
Suite 240
New York, NY 10011
USA
enslow.com

Published in 2016 by Enslow Publishing, LLC
101 W. 23rd Street, Suite 240, New York, NY 10011

**Library of Congress Cataloging-in-Publication Data**
Malaspina, Ann, 1957-
  Mao Zedong and the Chinese Revolution / Ann Malaspina.
    pages cm. — (People and events that changed the world)
  Includes bibliographical references and index.
  Audience: Grade 7 to 8.
  Audience: 12-up.
  ISBN 978-0-7660-7292-3
  1.  Mao, Zedong, 1893-1976—Juvenile literature. 2.  Revolutions—China—
History—20th century—Juvenile literature. 3.  Communism—China—History—
Juvenile literature. 4.  China—Politics and government—20th century—
Juvenile literature.  I. Title.
  DS778.M3M2353 2016
  951.04'2—dc23
                         2015031487

Printed in the United States of America

**To Our Readers:** We have done our best to make sure all website addresses in this book were active and appropriate when we went to press. However, the author and the publisher have no control over and assume no liability for the material available on those websites or on any websites they may link to. Any comments or suggestions can be sent by e-mail to customerservice@enslow.com.

Portions of this book originally appeared in the book *The Chinese Revolution and Mao Zedong in World History*.

# CONTENTS

Mao Zedong

# The Long March

China was in the grips of a long, bloody civil war in the autumn of 1934. The rebellious Red Army, representing the Communist Party of China, was battling the army loyal to the government. The Red Army was ill-equipped and disorganized, and its ragged troops were losing badly. The government's Chinese Nationalist Army, known as the Kuomintang, was stronger. Led by General Chiang Kai-shek, the soldiers were better trained and prepared. As the air grew colder, the Kuomintang surrounded the Communist stronghold in the southern province of Jiangxi. Desperate to escape, the Red Army started marching, first to the west, and then turning north. In October 1934, the Long March had begun.

## A Strong Leader

Some eighty-six thousand Communist soldiers and supporters set forth on the march that would change the course of China's history. Leading the First Army Unit of the Red Army was a tall man with big ideas. His name was Mao Zedong

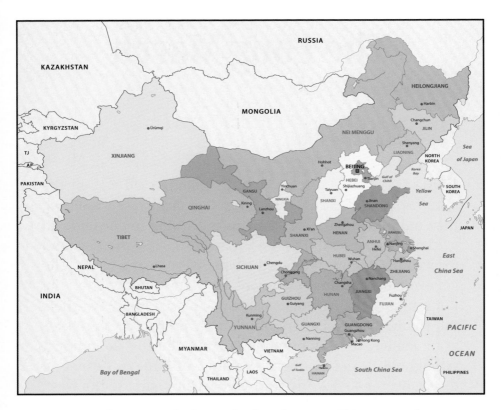

Mao Zedong's revolution took place in many Chinese provinces and cities. A map of modern-day China is shown here.

(also spelled Mao Tse-tung) and he was a strong leader. For him and other Communists, the civil war was a battle for the future of China. They wanted a country where the lines between the rich and the poor were erased, and private ownership of land and property was abolished. He dreamed of a China where peasants farmed their own land, and no one went hungry.

For eight months, the First Army Unit had been walking across the heart of China. By June 1935, they had reached the shadows of snow-covered Jiajin Mountain in Sichuan Province. The line of soldiers climbed a trail through the snow fields. Jiajin Mountain was called Fairy Mountain by the peasants in the region. They believed the towering peak was magical. The wind blew so cold, even in summer, that some people claimed the snow on the slopes had not melted for a thousand years.

Since it was summer in the valleys, the soldiers wore thin cotton clothing and sandals. Some were barefoot. The lucky ones wrapped themselves in fur they had stolen from Tibetan horsemen. The soldiers carried guns and supplies on their backs. The army cooks bent under the weight of packs carrying big bags of rice. However, there was little water to boil for meals, and the air was too thin to light fires.

The mountain was steep, but the soldiers moved forward. Mao, who was forty-one years old and physically strong, had little choice. To turn west would require confronting hostile Tibetan warriors. Kuomintang soldiers were gathered to the east. The only safe route to reach another Red Army unit, waiting with support, was to climb the mountain.

Many of Mao's soldiers had never seen snow. They wrapped their eyes in cloth to avoid snow blindness. They were told not to stop or they would risk frostbite. The path

This woodcut depicts the Chinese Red Army
during the Long March of 1934 and 1935.

disappeared after awhile, and some soldiers fell into icy gullies. Men slipped and shattered bones. Small avalanches spewed rocks and ice. Some who were already weak or ill did not survive. "We lost many good people. The weather was cold. Men froze to death. Some simply could not breath," one marcher told writer Harrison E. Salisbury.[1]

Most of the soldiers did survive Jiajin Mountain. Soon after, they met the Fourth Front Army in a small village. There some ten thousand people celebrated and feasted on food stolen from landlords. They paused to listen to Mao, who urged them to stay united and strong to fight the Japanese Army. The Japanese were gaining strength in China's north. There was no time to rest. More peaks in the Great Snowy Mountain range awaited.

The Long March began as a retreat, but built into a movement. The Red Army would prove its resilience and determination. More people were drawn to the Communist cause. The distance traveled is still uncertain. It may have been 7,767 miles (12,500 kilometers), as Mao later claimed, or half that amount as some researchers estimate. Despite the losses suffered by the Communists, Mao would consider the Long March a victory for himself and the Red Army. "The Long March is . . . a seeding-machine. In the eleven provinces it has sown many seeds which will sprout, leaf, blossom and bear fruit, and will yield a harvest in the future," he wrote later.[2] By the end of the march, Mao would emerge as the undisputed leader of the Communist Party. But the march was only the beginning. A long struggle lay ahead for Mao. The struggle would be even longer and more desperate for the Chinese people.

# CHAPTER 2

# Son of a Rice Farmer

Mao Zedong was born on December 26, 1893, into a China on the verge of collapse. The nation was in a sharp decline and the people were adrift in uncertainty. It is no wonder he would want to use his strong intellect and leadership abilities to forge a better future. Yet his childhood was more comfortable than most Chinese. He did not go to bed hungry. Mao was raised in security and tradition. As a child, he had little knowledge of China's problems and did not experience the hard life of the typical Chinese peasant.

For many generations, Mao's family had lived in his birthplace in the remote farming valley of Shaoshan, deep in the heart of Hunan Province in south-central China. Hunan contained fertile hills and valleys of tea plantations, bamboo groves, and rice fields. Without a river, Shaoshan was cut off from the rest of the world. As one writer noted, in Mao's day, no roads led to Shaoshan, only stony paths.

## A Comfortable Childhood

Daily life in Shaoshan had not changed much in hundreds of years. World events and politics seemed far away, while family relationships were most important. Chinese peasants depended on good harvests. When droughts came, they could not pay the high rent and taxes due to the landlords. Famines frequently swept through rural villages.

The Mao family relied on the rice harvest. However, they were fortunate to own land, instead of rent it from a landlord. Mao grew up in a comfortable farmhouse with a courtyard and tiled roof. Following the Chinese tradition, Mao was his family name and Zedong was the name given to him by his parents. His father and mother, Mao Yichang and Wen Qimei, had seven children—two daughters and five sons—but only three boys survived childhood. Zedong's brothers, Mao Zemin and Mao Zetan, would join the Communist revolution. Later, the family adopted a girl named Mao Zehong.

Zedong, the eldest child, was very fond and respectful of his mother. Wen Qimei was a devout Buddhist with a gentle, tolerant nature. Although her husband was a "skeptic" and did not follow any religion, she gave her children religious instruction.

His mother, like most Chinese at the time, was illiterate. She wanted more for her sons. Zedong went to work in the fields when he was just six years old. Two years later, he was enrolled in the primary school in Shaoshan. There, Zedong learned to read and write Chinese. This was a challenge since Chinese writing uses fifty thousand characters, rather than twenty-six letters. Each character represents a word. A person needs to know about two thousand characters in order to read Chinese comfortably. Zedong's success in learning to read and write would set him apart from the majority of Chinese.

Zedong was born in this house in the remote
city of Shaoshan in Hunan province.

## Zedong's Education

Zedong also studied the Chinese classics, or the ancient
texts on Chinese government and culture, required by the
schools. He read works by the great Chinese philosophers,
including Confucius. The teachings of Confucius, who
died in 479 BC, formed the basis for Chinese culture and
behavior for centuries. Confucius taught that families and
societies should be organized based on rules of behavior.
He considered benevolence the most important virtue. He
also valued loyalty, courage, wisdom, and trustworthiness.
Confucius felt that a nation's ruler should be like the father
of a family. The ruler should set a good moral example for
the people.

Zedong also learned about legalism, a political philosophy
founded by Han Fei, a rival of Confucius. In contrast to

# Primary Source: Zedong's Home Life

**My mother was a kind woman, generous and sympathetic, and ever ready to share what she had. She pitied the poor and often gave them rice when they came to ask for it during famines. But she could not do so when my father was present. He disapproved of charity. We had many quarrels in my home over this question.[1]**

Confucianism, legalism relies on the absolute, or total, power of the state. Human beings are considered selfish. Social order is preserved with strict laws and discipline. The ruler is all-powerful. Laws are tools to keep the people under control. Legalism became the form of rulership for some Chinese emperors, giving them absolute power. Those who disobeyed the emperor were severely punished.

Like many of his classmates, Zedong preferred fiction to the Chinese classics. He liked the romantic stories of Old China. These tales of heroes and revolts left a strong impression of the glory won by rebels. Zedong also found he had a talent for writing. He would become a prolific writer and poet.

Zedong's rebellious spirit was soon apparent. His teacher at the village school was strict and often beat the students. Unhappy at his treatment, one day when he was just ten years old, Zedong ran away from school, and his home. He wandered lost for three days before returning home. To his surprise, his teacher seemed to treat him with more respect afterward. "The result of my act of protest impressed me very much. It was a successful 'strike,'" he said later.[2]

Zedong's father expected his eldest son would one day inherit the farm. When Zedong was thirteen, Mao Yichang took him out of school. Zedong was to work the fields and keep the farm's business records. Zedong did not get along with his father, who had a strong temper. He was impatient with his restless, curious son. The two often fought and disagreed. Later, Zedong would criticize his father for being unsympathetic toward peasants.

Zedong was determined to resume his education. He managed to escape his chores in 1910 and hire two tutors in a nearby town. One of his tutors gave him a pamphlet called "The Dismemberment of China." It discussed how nations such as Japan and France had colonized Asia and dominated China.

## The Early History of China

During his studies, Zedong learned about China's great history. The Chinese call their country *Zhongguo*, which means "central land or the Middle Kingdom." The name reflects their belief that China is the center of the world and the only true civilization. In fact, Chinese have shared a common culture for longer than most other peoples. The Chinese have made important contributions to the world, including the art of papermaking, tea, gunpowder, silk cloth, and the compass.

The Chinese Empire was founded in 221 BC when a prince from the western state of Qin united seven warring states. Shi Huang Ti, meaning "First Emperor," formed the Qin Empire, the first of many Chinese dynasties, or ruling families. He standardized writing, currency, and weights

Zedong stands next to his father.

and measures. He established a government that built roads and palaces. However, Shi Huang Ti was a cruel ruler. He adopted the philosophy of legalism, rejecting the benevolent Confucian ideals. He persecuted the rich, burned books, and killed scholars. Dissent was not tolerated. Small crimes were punished by the loss of a hand or foot. He forced prisoners to build the Great Wall of China to keep out barbarians from the north. Mao came to admire the First Emperor after studying about him.

The Qin dynasty lasted only fourteen years. Rebellions by peasants and ministers ended the use of legalism as a state philosophy. The Qin dynasty was replaced by the more friendly Han dynasty. More empires followed. In 1644 Manchus from the northeast established the Qing dynasty. The Qing dynasty led China during three centuries of prosperity, stability, and expansion, but those good years eventually came to an end.

# China Struggles

China became isolated during the Qing dynasty. It fell behind the modernization and industrialization occurring in Western countries. When its isolation ended, new problems arose. By the mid-1800s, Europeans had discovered China's riches. They came to trade in China's tea, silk, porcelain, and other products. To balance the trade, they sold opium, an addictive drug, to the Chinese. The Qing emperor had banned the opium trade in 1800, but the foreigners ignored the ban. After the Chinese seized twenty thousand chests of British opium in Guangzhou, the British went on the attack.

The Opium War raged from 1839 to 1842. China was defeated and forced to establish seaports to receive foreign goods, such as imports of cheap cloth, which further damaged local economies. China also had to give the island of Hong Kong to Great Britain. As a British colony, Hong Kong became an important trade center. Under the terms of a ninety-nine year lease, Hong Kong was not returned to China until 1997.

Japan also posed a threat to China. The two countries were long rivals. Japan defeated China in the Sino-Japanese War of 1894 to 1895. Japan forced China to hand over Taiwan and other lands. Gradually, other countries dominated China, as well. Japanese and other foreigners were allowed to open factories in China. Germany, Britain, Russia, and France demanded that China hand over land. The foreign powers divided China into "spheres of influence," each dominated by one nation. Unable to resist, China fell into serious debt. The government raised taxes, making the Chinese people poor.

The imperial government did little to protect China. By this time, the Qing dynasty had become corrupt. To add to its difficulties, by 1850, China's population had grown to over 400 million people. China was the world's most populous country. This led to a shortage of jobs and low pay. The ordinary worker had a harder time making a living. Peasants had smaller farms to raise their food. Farmers overused their land, causing soil erosion. "Too many people trying to make a living on too few resources naturally also exacerbated social tensions," wrote Patricia Buckley Ebrey, in the *Cambridge Illustrated History of China*.[3]

# The Boxer Rebellion

In 1898 radical reformers urged the emperor, Guangxu, to modernize China and to change the structure of government and society. The emperor began issuing proclamations to bring change, but he had little influence. His aunt, the Empress Dowager Cixi, held the reigns of power, and she was against the reforms. She executed many of the radicals, putting a temporary stop to the movement for change.

Unrest swept through China in 1899 and 1900. A secret society of peasants from the north organized to oppose Western imperialism. The society was called the "Righteous and Harmonious Fists"; the Europeans called them the Boxers because of their martial arts skills. The Boxers wanted to expel foreigners and foreign influence from China. They resented the missionaries who were converting the Chinese to Christianity.

Supported by the empress and the government, the Boxers burned down churches and houses of Westerners, and killed Chinese Christians. By June 1900, the Boxers occupied Beijing and Tianjin. The Western countries fought back. In August 1900, a coalition of British, French, Russian, American, German, and Japanese soldiers fought their way into Beijing. The troops, numbering nearly twenty thousand, defeated the Boxers, and the empress fled the city. To settle the conflict, China had to pay heavy fines, sign treaties favoring the foreign countries, and allow foreign troops into Beijing. The foreigners saw China as a barbaric country. The Boxer Rebellion's bitter aftermath fueled frustration among the Chinese people. More than ever, they wanted China's independence.

## The Seeds of a Philosophy

Zedong was aware of injustices close to home. When he was young, a famine devastated Changsha, the provincial capital, and thousands were starving. "The starving sent a delegation to the civil governor to beg for relief, but he

A group of Catholics prepare to defend themselves during the Boxer Rebellion. The Chinese peasants were trying to rid their country of all Western influences, including Christianity, but were ultimately defeated by a coalition of Americans and Europeans.

replied to them haughtily, 'Why haven't you food? There is plenty in the city. I always have enough,'" Mao recalled later. The people organized a demonstration and drove out the governor. A new governor arrested the rebel leaders. Many protestors were beheaded and their heads were displayed in public. "I never forgot it. I felt that there with the rebels were ordinary people like my own family and I deeply resented the injustice of the treatment given to them," said Mao.[4]

In 1910 Zedong enrolled in a school in a nearby market town, Xiangxiang. The school offered classes in science and Western ideas. For the first time, Zedong learned about world events. Eager to see what lay beyond his home, Zedong enrolled in a school in Changsha. He was seventeen when he is said to have walked thirty miles to Changsha. In Changsha, Zedong began exploring ideas that would later develop into his political philosophy.

While Zedong's life led him far from Shaoshan, he never forgot his early years. "It was there that Mao had hammered out his own revolutionary philosophy, a philosophy steeped in knowledge of the Chinese peasant and the countryside," wrote Harrison E. Salisbury.[5] Mao's knowledge of the simple life of the Chinese peasant would form the basis of his political ideas. (Much later, his bodyguards would use the nickname "the Old Peasant" to refer to Mao. Yet some would doubt that he really understood their harsh lives.) Discontent and new ideas were sweeping across China, and Mao was taken by the tide.

# Uprising

The Chinese were impatient for change and new leadership after the disaster of the Boxer Rebellion. The emperor's government in Beijing had not given up its reign. Indeed, the Qing dynasty tried desperately to hold on. They tried to rebuild the military, boost up trade and industry, and reach out to the provinces. But the twentieth century was beginning. The rest of the world was changing fast, and the time of the emperors had passed. The people of China wanted a government that would listen to their needs. They wanted leaders that would not be held back by traditional assumptions and ancient ways.

## Sun Yat-sen

The movement for a republican government, or a government run by the people, found a spokesman in Sun Yat-sen. Sun was a doctor who had spent much of his life outside China. He was born in 1866 to a farming family in southeast China. He studied in missionary schools in Honolulu, Hawaii. He later went to Hong Kong, where he trained as a physician. Sun also converted to Christianity. He practiced medicine only briefly, for he was more interested in shaping China's future. Like other revolutionaries of his time, Sun wanted to free China of foreign control and overthrow the Qing dynasty.

After he returned to China, in the mid-1890s, Sun led an unsuccessful revolt against the imperial government. Sun was a skilled leader who drew many people together behind the common goal of ending China's imperial rule. In 1905, while in exile in Japan, Sun founded the United League, China's first modern revolutionary organization. Most members of the group were Chinese living overseas.

Sun's political theory included the "Three People's Principles," a combination of nationalism, democracy, and socialism. Nationalism is a philosophy in which a person's loyalty is to the nation; one's nation is considered superior to other nations. In a democracy, the government is run by and for the people. Socialism is a system in which the means of production is shared by everyone in common ownership; everyone has an equal share in the goods produced, even though each person may not produce the same amount of goods. Sun thought China had to go through stages to reach a democracy. He also sought a strong central government to protect China from exploitation.

## Toppling a Dynasty

It took years of struggle by Sun and other republican revolutionaries to topple the Qing dynasty. Many uprisings failed. Meanwhile, the empire grew weaker. In 1908 the Qing Empress Dowager Cixi and Emperor Guangxu both died within days of each other. The last Chinese emperor, Pu Yi, a three-year-old boy, ascended the throne.

Sun Yat-sen, pictured here in 1912, was a revolutionary whose philosophy was a combination of nationalism, democracy, and socialism.

Sun Yat-sen was in the United States, gathering support for his revolution, when an anti-Manchu organization of Chinese troops rose on October 10, 1911. The rebels took over Wuhan, an industrial center on the Middle Yangtze River. Overpowered, the Manchus were defeated. On January 1, 1912, Sun was inaugurated as provisional president of the Republic of China in the city of Nanjing. Yet Sun lacked the power and foreign support to unify China. He gave the presidency to Yuan Shikai, a military leader in northern China.

The Qing Empire officially came to an end on February 12, 1912, when the emperor Pu Yi gave up his title. Just seven years old, Pu Yi was allowed to live on in the Imperial City in Beijing. In 1924 a warlord expelled him from the palace and he took refuge with the Japanese. In 1934 he was given the title of emperor of Manchuria by the occupying Japanese army and ruled until 1945.

# The Warlords

Yuan Shikai, president of China in 1912, quickly proved no better than an emperor. He used the military to gain power for himself. Soon he was a dictator. Outraged, Sun Yat-sen and others organized a new political party. Founded in 1912, the Kuomintang, or the National People's Party, sought to unite China and provide economic security for the people. The Kuomintang won the majority in national parliamentary elections in the next years. Yuan suppressed the Kuomintang and Sun fled to Japan, but the party still gained support in parts of China.

China's condition soon worsened. After Yuan's death in 1916, China broke up into warring regions. The regions were led by warlords, or military leaders who used violent force to control their kingdoms. The warlord era was a period of violence, oppression, and disunity. Military strength replaced political authority. The peasants paid high taxes to support the warlords. China fell into more foreign debt. It was on this canvas that China's youth and intellectuals painted a revolution of new ideas.

## Student Protests

The revolution of ideas was sparked, in part, by events outside China. During Yuan's rule, World War I broke out in June 1914. The war began when an assassin gunned down Archduke Franz Ferdinand of Austria-Hungary in Sarajevo, the capital of Austria-Hungary's province of Bosnia-Herzegovina. During WWI, which lasted from 1914 to 1918, China joined the Allies—which included the United States, France, and Great Britain—against Germany. Chinese soldiers did not go to battle, but thousands of Chinese laborers worked in France behind the lines. The Allies defeated Germany.

At the war's end, China expected to recover its land from foreign occupiers. This included Shandong, a coastal Chinese province controlled by Germany. Unexpectedly, during the Paris Peace Conference, the Allies gave Shandong to Japan. The Chinese felt betrayed. This event added to growing discontent among young people.

Discontent grew into a movement for change. On May 4, 1919, three thousand college students marched into Tiananmen Square in Beijing to protest China's treatment by the Allies. The students and intellectuals called on China to embrace progress, democracy, and science. They urged China to move away from its old ways. This was called the May Fourth Movement.

Students from Peking University march in protest of China's treatment by the Allied forces after World War I. The protest, which took place on May 4, 1919, was part of a series of demonstrations that are known as the May Fourth Movement.

## Mao the Writer

Like many young men, Mao Zedong joined Sun Yat-sen's Republican army in 1911. He spent six months in the army, but he never saw combat. Instead, he stayed on duty in the army garrison in Changsha. He wrote letters for men in his squad. "I could write, I knew something about books, and they respected my 'great learning,'" recalled Mao.[1]

After the Qing dynasty collapsed, Mao returned to his studies. In 1912 he enrolled in a traditional school in Changsha, where he read Chinese history. He soon left to study alone in the local library. There, he discovered Western classics such as Adam Smith's *The Wealth of Nations*, Darwin's *On the Origin of Species*, and Herbert Spencer's *Logic*. He also read the work of Western political philosophers.

In 1913 Mao enrolled in the Hunan First Normal School, where his teacher, Yang Changji, became an important influence. Yang advocated combining Western science with Chinese culture. "He taught ethics, he was an idealist and a man of high moral character. He believed in his ethics very strongly and tried to imbue his students with the desire to become just, moral, virtuous men, useful in society," Mao said.[2]

## "We Are Awakened!"

After graduating from teachers' college in 1918, Mao moved to Beijing. He took a clerical job at the Beijing University library. The head librarian, Li Dazhao, became Mao's mentor, or teacher. Mao returned to Changsha in 1919 and became involved in political activity supporting the May Fourth Movement. He got students to protest the Allied leaders and boycott Japanese goods. He also published *New Hunan*, a magazine that supported the May Fourth Movement. After the governor banned the magazine, Mao led protestors to Beijing to demand that the governor be removed from office.

Mao wrote articles for the magazine, *New Youth*, which was founded in 1915 by Chen Duxiu, the radical intellectual who led the May Fourth Movement. His first article in described a personal fitness program for Chinese to follow in order to become military heroes. In other articles, Mao criticized Confucianism. He urged people to rise up against old traditions. "We are awakened! The world is ours, the nation is ours, society is ours. If we do not speak, who will speak? If we do not act, who will act? If we do not rise up and fight, who will rise up and fight?" he wrote in 1919.[3]

In 1920, Mao married Yang Kaihui, the daughter of his teacher, Yang Changji. Mao had been married as a young teenager. His father had arranged a union between him and a local village girl, but Mao did not recognize that first arranged marriage. Yang and Mao had three sons: Mao Anying, Mao Anqing, and Mao Anlong.

# A New Philosophy

Mao began to read about Communism, a political philosophy attracting interest among Chinese intellectuals. Communism is based on the ideas of Karl Marx and Friedrich Engels. In 1848, the two German philosophers published *The Communist Manifesto*. They wrote about transforming society by abolishing social classes. The major resources and means of production would be owned by the state. Private property would not exist. In theory, everybody would share all work, according to their abilities, and everybody would benefit, according to their needs. The state would be responsible for taking care of the people. Communism would create a more just and equal society. Marx and Engels predicted it would liberate the members of the proletariat, or working class, who work for low pay in the factories of Europe.

Mao read many books about Communism. These books "especially deeply carved my mind, and built up in me a faith in Marxism, from which . . . I did not afterwards waver," he told Edgar Snow. "By the summer of 1920 I had become, in theory and to some extent in action, a Marxist, and from this time on I considered myself a Marxist."[4]

German philosophers Karl Marx and Friedrich Engels, illustrated here, set down their views of a Communist society without classes, private property, or state in *The Communist Manifesto*, published in 1848.

# Fall of the Tsars

By 1920 Communism had already toppled the tsars of Russia. The tsars were similar to the Chinese emperors. For many centuries, Russia had been led by tsarist regimes. While living in luxury, the tsars allowed their people little freedom or the means to escape from poverty. Many Russians felt that Communism was a better alternative. Russian Communists overthrew Tsar Nicholas II in the October Revolution of 1917 and seized power. The revolutionaries, known as Bolsheviks, were led by Vladimir Ilich Lenin, the founder of the Communist Party in Russia.

A brilliant intellectual, trained as a lawyer, Lenin suffered under the tsarist regime. He was exiled for revolutionary activity. Lenin was determined to bring change to Russia. He transformed Marx's ideas into a political revolution. Marx thought that workers and peasants would carry out

# Primary Source:
## *The Communist Manifesto*

The Communists disdain to conceal their views and aims. They openly declare that their ends can be attained only by the forcible overthrow of all existing social conditions. Let the ruling classes tremble at a Communistic revolution. The proletarians have nothing to lose but their chains. They have a world to win.

Working men of all countries unite![5]

the revolution on their own. Lenin maintained that a small group of leaders should lead the revolution. He often called it "the dictatorship of the proletariat," which meant the Bolshevik party would impose its doctrines on all of Russia. Later, China would adopt Lenin's idea of rule by a select few.

Lenin set up a dictatorship, using terror and force to carry out his vision. He routed out his enemies with a secret police force. He even imposed artificial famines to erase opposition. "Within months of taking power, Lenin liquidated the fragile legal system that had been in place . . . and commenced a system of state terror that was designated to intimidate the population and ensure the survival of the regime," wrote Soviet expert David Remnick.[6] In other words, Lenin would not allow criticism.

## Chinese Communism

In 1921 a group of scholars secretly organized the Chinese Communist Party in Shanghai. Mao's mentor, Li Dazhao, along with Chen Duxiu, were the two founding fathers. On July 21, 1921, Mao, at the age of twenty-seven, led the Hunan delegation to the First Congress of the Chinese Communist Party in Shanghai. At this first meeting of the Chinese Communist Party, Mao was named secretary of the Hunan branch of the party. Advisors from Comintern, or Communist International, a group that spread Communism beyond Russia's borders, helped advise the party.

China and Russia shared an important feature. The peasants and workers in Russia and China had labored for centuries under tsars and emperors, respectively. In China, the warlord era had left the peasants worse off than ever. Communism held out the promise that people would share in the nation's wealth and avoid starvation.

31

CHAPTER 4

# The Red Army

**M**ao and his comrades faced many obstacles in their effort to spread Communism in China. One of the most difficult obstacles was the military commander and politician Chiang Kai-shek. At first, he was Mao's rival. Later, Chiang was Mao's arch enemy. Like Mao, Chiang wanted to lead China into the future, but the two men had very different ideas and values. Chiang was not as interested in gaining the support of the peasants. He wanted to build up bases in the cities and to establish China as a world power. He did not believe in Communism. In the end, the two men's struggle against each other to win China would tear the country apart.

For a time, Mao and Chiang shared a common goal. For China to move forward, the warlords had to be defeated and the country had to be united. The Soviet Union, which was the new name taken by Russia in 1922, urged the Chinese Communist Party to join with the Kuomintang, or National People's Party, which was gaining strength in many provinces. Together, the two groups would have a better chance of bringing the country together under a republican government. In 1923 the Kuomintang leader Sun Yat-sen agreed to form the United Front with the Communists. For several years, the two groups fought to destroy the warlord's stronghold on China.

# A Skillful Leader

Like Mao, Chiang Kai-shek came from modest, rural roots. He was born on October 11, 1887, in Fenghua, a remote farm village in Zhejiang, an eastern province of China. His father earned a living as a salt seller. As a young man, Chiang left China to train at a military academy in Tokyo, Japan, in 1907, where he met Sun. Chiang returned to China in 1911 to join Sun in the overthrow of the imperial government.

Chiang also received military training in Moscow. He was then named commandant of the training center for Kuomintang soldiers. Chiang became commander in chief of the Kuomintang's White Army. When Sun Yat-sen died in 1925, Chiang was the natural choice to lead the party.

# Chiang versus the Communists

Chiang's military prowess offered new hope in the unification of China. In 1926, with Communist support, Chiang embarked on the Northern Expedition to fight the warlords. At that time, the Kuomintang controlled only two provinces. To divert attention, Communist rebels incited strikes and upheaval in southeastern China. By March 1927, the Kuomintang armies had pushed back the warlords and taken all of southeastern China.

Unlike Sun Yat-sen, Chiang was not willing to share his revolution with the Communists. He was convinced they were disruptive and posed a threat to his authority. By 1927 Chiang had decided that the Communists were enemies, rather than friends. Chiang set out to destroy the Communist strongholds.

The Nationalist leader Chiang Kai-shek posed the most
serious challenge to Mao's victory over China.

At dawn on April 12, 1927, Kuomintang troops surrounded Communist-held areas in Shanghai, the port city on the East China Sea. Shanghai was a crowded and bustling trading center. Half the city was dominated by foreigners and foreign businesses. The Chinese side of Shanghai was poor and working-class. Many Chinese workers were members of unions and sympathetic to the Communists.

The White Army of the Kuomintang staged its attack in the working-class areas. Taken by surprise, some four hundred Communist sympathizers were killed. Zhou Enlai, the top Communist Party official in Shanghai, ordered a general strike of workers the next day. Then about one thousand workers, including women and children who worked in the textile mills, marched to the military headquarters to hand in a petition about the strike. Kuomintang soldiers fired on the unarmed protestors. Many were killed, and more were wounded. Thousands of Communists were killed in what is known as the "White Terror."

In other provinces, the Kuomintang were capturing and executing Communists. In May 1927, fighting erupted in Changsha. An estimated ten thousand people died. Communists and even suspected Communists were executed by the Kuomintang. In another province, Hubei, thousands of villagers were slaughtered.

## Organizing Peasants

Like many Communists, Mao cooperated for a time with the Kuomintang. He held important positions in the governing committee of the party. As relations between the two groups broke down, Mao was removed from those positions. Meanwhile, he was busy organizing peasants in Hunan, his home province.

Life was a struggle for China's peasants, who comprised about 80 percent of the population. Droughts, floods, and famine were common. They paid high taxes and saw little profit from their hard work. Mao sought to harness their dissatisfaction. Mao wanted, not just to improve the peasants' lives, but to gain their loyalty in a Communist revolution. In 1926 Mao researched peasants living near Changsha. In his historic document, "Report on an Investigation of the Peasant Movement in Hunan," Mao stated that peasants would be a major force in a revolution.

Despite Mao's efforts, peasant support of the Communists was dwindling. Many had been killed. Others were afraid of opposing Chiang's army. Humiliated by many defeats, on August 1, 1927, the Communist leader Zhou Enlai ordered Communists to rise up against the Kuomintang in Nanchang. The Communists won a victory with few shots fired.

The Nanchang Uprising is celebrated as the establishment of the Communist's Red Army. Mao realized that a strong army was necessary to achieve political ideals. "From now on, we should pay the greatest attention to military affairs. We must know that political power is obtained from the barrel of the gun," Mao wrote in August 1927.[1]

## Communists Retreat

Still, the Communists could not defeat the Kuomintang. In the fall of 1927, Mao helped organize an unsuccessful uprising in Changsha. The Autumn Harvest Uprising, as it was known, was a disaster for the Communists and Mao, who was expelled from the central committee of the Communist Party. The Communists retreated to the countryside. By year's end, party membership had fallen drastically. In 1928 Chiang's troops captured Beijing.

# Primary Source: The Chinese Peasants

The poor peasants are tenant-peasants who are exploited by the landlords. They may again be divided into two categories according to their economic status. One category has comparatively adequate farm implements and some funds. Such peasants may retain half the product of their year's toil. To make up their deficit they cultivate side crops, catch fish or shrimps, raise poultry or pigs, or sell part of their labour power, and thus eke out a living, hoping in the midst of hardship and destitution to tide over the year. Thus their life is harder than that of the semi-owner peasants, but they are better off than the other category of poor peasants. They ate more revolutionary than the semi-owner peasants, but less revolutionary than the other category of poor peasants. As for the latter, they have neither adequate farm implements nor funds nor enough manure, their crops are poor, and, with little left after paying rent, they have even greater need to sell part of their labour power. In hard times they piteously beg help from relatives and friends, borrowing a few *tou* or *sheng* of grain to last them a few days, and their debts pile up like loads on the backs of oxen. They are the worst off among the peasants and are highly receptive to revolutionary propaganda.

–This quote from Mao's "Analysis of the Classes in Chinese Society," written in 1926, shows how he saw the poor Chinese peasants as ready for revolution. [2]

For now, the Communists were defeated. The Kuomintang had overwhelmed the warlords, crushed the Communists, and reunited the country. The national government was moved to Nanjing. From 1928 to 1937, the Kuomintang controlled much of China. They made some reforms, but the lives of the peasants did not improve much. With a stronger leadership, China began regaining its autonomy, or independence. Foreign countries recognized Chiang Kai-shek's government.

## Winning the Peasants

Mao and the Red Army soldiers were forced to flee to the countryside. Mao settled in the mountains of south China where he established the Jiangxi Soviet. He created a Soviet-style government and built up the Red Army. Rather than capturing cities, as the Soviet advisers urged, Mao focused on gaining peasant support. Mao took land from landlords and gave it to the peasants. In doing so, he won over more peasants. By 1930 Mao was acting independently from the Soviets. In three years, the Jiangxi Soviet grew rapidly; the Red Army grew, as well.

Mao had an able assistant, Zhu De. Zhu was a talented military leader. He had been a warlord in the 1920s and an opium addict. But he fought his opium addiction and put aside his wealth to join the Communist Party. Zhu was skilled at the art of war and a natural leader. The men who followed Zhu into battle adored him. Zhu often went without shoes to share hardships with his men.

## The Red Army

Zhu led an army of volunteer soldiers from across China. Some were as young as fourteen years old. Many were farm laborers and craftsmen. Only a few were merchants and intellectuals. They were paid by income from their land or public land taken from landlords. As journalist Edgar Snow wrote, "I soon discovered that the great mass of the Red soldiery was made up of young peasants and workers who believed themselves to be fighting for their homes, their land, and their country."[3] The Red Army officers were only in their mid-twenties. Some had graduated from military academies in the Soviet Union.

Under the officers' command, the army developed its unique fighting style. The army would build up peasant support in the countryside, then encircle cities and close in on the Kuomintang. The army's meager supply of weapons was mostly captured from the enemy. Without professional training, and lacking supplies and arms, the Red Army developed the tactics of guerrilla warfare. Instead of attacking head-on, they used knowledge of local terrain to ambush the enemy, then quickly retreat. Mao later wrote:

> When the invader pierces deep into the heart of the weaker country and occupies her territory in a cruel and oppressive manner, there is no doubt that conditions of terrain, climate, and society in general offer obstacles to his progress and may be used to advantage by those who oppose him. In guerrilla warfare we turn these advantages to the purpose of resisting and defeating the enemy. . .[4]

The Red Army set out to win the loyalty of the peasants. The soldiers were told to take nothing from them and to pay fairly for food and clothing. Thus, tens of thousands of peasants pledged their allegiance to the Communists. These

Mao is shown here wearing the cap with a red star that was part of the uniform of the Red Army.

tactics were encouraged by Mao. "Modern warfare is not a matter in which armies alone can determine victory or defeat. Especially in guerrilla combat, we must rely on the force of the popular masses, for it is only thus that we can have a guarantee of success," Mao wrote in 1937.[5]

## Heavy Losses

In 1930, Mao's Red Army captured Changsha, then withdrew. A second assault on Changsha was a disaster. The Communists suffered heavy losses. In November 1930, two months after the failed attack, Mao's wife, Yang Kaihui, was beheaded on the orders of the governor. Their children were hidden by relatives and secretly sent to Shanghai. A few months later, the youngest, Anlong, died of a disease called dysentery. Kuomintang soldiers dug up the graves of Mao's parents, according to one account. These attacks on Mao Zedong's family indicated that the Kuomintang considered him one of its chief enemies.

# Primary Source: Mao's Poetry

**The enemy advances, we retreat.**
**The enemy halts, we move in.**
**The enemy tires, we attack.**
**The enemy retreats, we pursue.**[6]

*—Mao made the Red Army learn this four-line poem, which is made up of sixteen Chinese characters. The poem rhymes in the original Chinese.*

Despite these tragedies, Mao was gaining strength as a leader. In 1931 the All-China Congress of Chinese Soviets elected Mao as chairman of the first All-China Soviet Government. Zhu De was elected as the military commander. (Mao would be reelected in 1934 at the Second All-China Soviet Congress.) However, a famine in northwest China from 1929 to 1931 had killed between five and ten million people, adding to the hardships endured by China's peasants.

Chiang Kai-shek's rule was never complete. Many areas lay beyond the reach of the nationalists. Still, by 1934 the White Army surrounded the Red Army in Jiangxi Province, the Communist stronghold. In a desperate flight for safety, Communists began to march, first west, and then turning to the north. The Communists needed to find a new base. They needed an area to call their own.

# A New Leader

The Long March would be a trial of endurance for the Red Army and an opportunity for Mao to secure his position as a commander. The many kilometers that lay ahead for the poorly-equipped soldiers were an important test for Mao. Already a Communist chief, he still had to prove his ability to lead his people. Not only did he have to be strong enough to endure harsh weather and terrain, and long distances on foot, but he had to show a practical ability to plan routes and make decisions. After all, the march was a retreat from the stronger Kuomintang. Mao would need sharp wits to turn the retreat into a victory, and not a disaster.

On October 18, 1934, Mao and his pregnant wife, a revolutionary named He Zizhen, joined some eighty-six thousand Communist soldiers and supporters. The couple left their two-year-old son, Anhong, with Mao's brother, Mao Zetan, who was staying with the rearguard group. Zetan later left the boy with a bodyguard. Anhong was never seen by his parents again.

## The Long March

The Red Army lugged weapons, food, maps, printing presses, and other heavy equipment. They marched single file over

Mao (right) stands next to his third wife, He Zizhen, who was also a revolutionary and a skilled fighter.

stone paths crossing hills and rice paddies. On their long retreat, the soldiers crossed rivers and scaled mountains, staying out of sight on the plains and roads. Mao and the other leaders stayed up nights to plan tactics for the next day.

The Communists met disaster in late November when they tried to cross the Xiang River in the north of Guangxi Province. The Red Army had to face both the White Army as well as the local warlord. They battled through barbed wire and concrete blockhouses. Outgunned by machine gun artillery, the Red soldiers suffered heavy casualties. According to eyewitness accounts, the Xiang River flowed red with blood and bodies. During the week it took the Red Army to cross the river, the Communists lost fifty thousand men.

After this episode, the Red Army dropped some of its supplies in order to move faster. Yet they were unsure where they were headed. In January 1935, the battered guerrillas were able to seize the city of Zunyi in Guizhou Province. In Zunyi, Communist Party leaders met in a major conference to discuss the war. During the meeting, Mao voiced criticisms of the military action as planned by the Soviet-backed party leadership. Mao suggested that the army use unconventional guerrilla tactics. Zhou Enlai, a respected military commander, proposed that Mao take over army leadership. Zhou became one of Mao's most trusted subordinates for decades to come. Mao did not receive formal leadership of the Chinese Communist Party until 1943, but he was now considered the leader of both the Communist Party and the Red Army.

# Frostbite and Despair

Mao decided the march should not be a retreat. Instead, it became a crusade north to fight the Japanese. The Japanese Army had invaded northern China in the early 1930s and was moving south. "March north to fight Japan!" became the slogan of the Long March. From then on, the army did not march in a straight line or in one body. Several columns would zigzag and backtrack to keep the White Army unsure of the Red Army's location. Not every Communist commander followed Mao. Some men broke off to establish their own bases.

Many obstacles lay ahead. Kuomintang troops and local warlords prevented the Red Army from crossing the Yangtze River. So the Communists were unable to establish a base in Sichuan Province, as they had hoped. Instead, they were forced to turn south to escape. They then headed north, staying close to the Tibetan border. Their final destination was the northern province of Shaanxi.

The Red Army walked many miles every day. Cold, hunger, and disease killed many of the marchers. Without adequate food, they foraged for weeds and berries. They suffered from malnutrition, frostbite, and despair.

# The End of the March

One of the Red Army's most daring feats occurred in May 1935. The Red Army needed to cross the Dadu River in Sichuan Province. There were not enough ferry boats where they needed to cross. One unit was ordered to go one hundred miles upstream to Luding. In Luding, a long narrow bridge, made of iron links and wooden planking, crossed the river. The bridge was controlled by Kuomintang

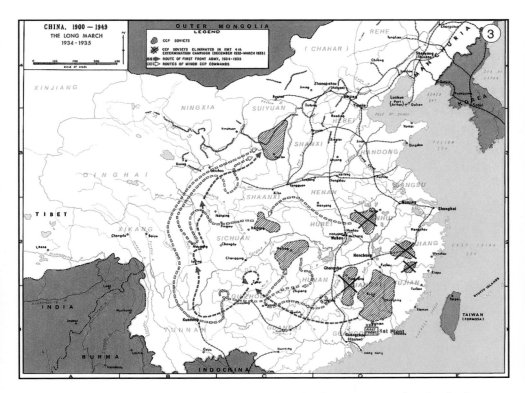

This map shows the various routes taken in the Long March. The darker dotted line represents the marches of the Red Army.

soldiers on the other side. "One by one Red soldiers stepped forward to risk their lives . . . Hand grenades and Mausers [a type of rifle] were strapped to their backs, and soon they were swinging out above the boiling river, moving hand over hand, clinging to the iron chains," wrote Edgar Snow.[1] The Kuomintang removed the wooden floor planks on one side. They fired at the Red Army, and set fire to the planks. The Red Army put out the fires. All but a few soldiers made it to the other shore.

Many miles lay ahead. The army climbed the icy peaks of the Great Snowy Mountains. Bombing raids by the Kuomintang Air Force injured Mao's wife, He Zizhen, and others. Later, they crossed the treacherous grasslands. Men sank in the mud and were sickened from eating raw vegetables.

In October 1935, Mao and his soldiers straggled into Wayaboa in Shaanxi Province, just south of the Great Wall. The Long March was over. Historians estimate that about eight thousand marchers reached Shaanxi Province, where they were joined by thousands of Communist soldiers and supporters. Many thousands had been lost, some dead and others injured or deserted, in the six-thousand-mile march. It hardly seemed a victory, yet by surviving the ordeal, the Communists gained hope that one day they would prevail in China. Importantly, the Long March established Mao as the Communist leader.

# Political Leader

At first, Mao led the Communist movement from a cave in a hillside village, Bao'an. He was thin and gaunt, and his life was in upheaval. His brother, Mao Zetan, was killed in combat in 1935. Mao Zedong and his wife, He Zizhen, had lost two children: Their two-year-old son and a newborn daughter were left with peasant families and never seen again. He Zizhen was still recovering from shrapnel injuries. She soon gave birth to another girl, Li Min. But Mao's wife became unhappy. She decided to leave China for the Soviet Union to have the shrapnel removed. While being treated in the Soviet Union, she gave birth to a son, who died at the age of ten months.

**Mao Zedong stands with his political chief Zhou Enlai (left) and his military commander Zhu De (right) on the Long March.**

With his wife gone, Mao fell in love with another woman. In 1939, Mao married Jiang Qing, a Shanghai actress twenty-one years younger than himself. Mao and Jiang Qing had a daughter, Li Na, who was born in 1940. Meanwhile, Mao made the transformation from revolutionary guerrilla to political leader.

## Maoism

The Communist leaders soon left the caves and moved to Yan'an, about sixty miles away. Yan'an was a market town

# Primary Source: The Long March

The Red Army fears not the trials of the Long March
And thinks nothing of a thousand mountains and rivers.
The Wuling Ridges spread out like ripples;
The Wumeng Ranges roll like balls of clay.
Warmly are the cliffs wrapped in clouds washed by
    the Gold Sand;
Chilly are the iron chains lying across the width of
    the Great Ferry.
A thousand acres of snow on the Min Mountain delight
My troops who have just left them behind.[2]

*—Mao Zedong wrote this poem about the Red Army's
  victory at the Luding Bridge.*

where traders brought timber, salt, and other goods to sell. Above the town towered a white pagoda. It became a symbol for the young people who walked hundreds of miles to Yan'an to join the revolution. The Communist rebels went to work. Small industries were launched, and fields were planted.

Mao occupied a merchant's house on the slopes of a mountain. He spent his days and nights studying and writing. He was forming ideas about China's future. Mao wanted to free China from the grasp of foreign powers. He wanted a new system of government and a new social structure. Gradually, he developed a political philosophy known as Maoism. It was a combination of Marxism and socialistic thought, adapted to the people and conditions of China.

Marx had glorified industrial workers as the leaders of the Socialist revolution. In the Soviet Union, Lenin led a revolution in cities for the workers in factories and industries. In contrast, Mao sought to harness the support, and change the lives, of rural peasants. Mao also advocated the idea of perpetual, or continuous, revolution. By this, Mao meant that revolution was a process that was always occurring.

Mao believed in class struggle, or the conflict between the peasants and the wealthy. In Mao's view, every person was born into a class. "In class society everyone lives as a member of a particular class, and every kind of thinking, without exception, is stamped with the brand of a class," he wrote in 1937.[3] If a person's grandfather was a landlord, then he or she belonged to the landlord class, even if the land was lost. Mao resented landlords and other members of the wealthy class. They had oppressed the peasants for too long. It was time for the peasants to rise up.

Mao wrote long essays about his ideas. Followers of Mao carried copies of the essays in their pockets. They studied his words, day and night, memorizing every phrase. More and more people were drawn to his ideas.

In Yan'an, Mao built his political power to ensure that he would be the man to lead China. He surrounded himself with trusted friends such as Deng Xiaoping, Lin Biao, and other loyal Communists. Some of his comrades began rewriting the history of China to make Mao the center of it. It was a hint of the godlike role to which Mao aspired. Mao also began to punish people whose loyalty to Communism was in doubt. Thousands of people were persecuted for betraying the ideas of the Communist Party.

# War With Japan

Meanwhile, Japanese aggression cast a darkening shadow. Japan was interested in the northern Chinese province of Manchuria, which was rich in minerals and other natural resources. A bomb of unknown origin blew up the Japanese railway near Shenyang, Manchuria, in September 1931. The Japanese Army used the incident to justify occupying southern Manchuria. By February 1932, the Japanese Army occupied all of Manchuria. Japan proclaimed it the state of Manchukuo. Japanese soldiers and settlers took over businesses and moved into private homes.

As the Communists built strength in Shaanxi, the Japanese Army was moving south. The Communists could not fight the Japanese on their own. They felt the Kuomintang government was not doing enough to stop the Japanese. Even the Kuomintang soldiers perceived the danger of losing to Japan. In December 1936, one of Chiang Kai-shek's generals kidnapped him. As a condition of his release, he agreed to join with the Communists. Thus, the Kuomintang and the Communists formed the United Front against Japan. Still, the two never trusted each other. Fighting continued to erupt between them. Mao's brother, Mao Zemin, who had made the Long March, was killed in 1942, in an anti-Communist purge in Sinkiang.

A full-scale war between China and Japan broke out in 1937. The Japanese Army set out to conquer cities, roads, and railroads. The Chinese Army, under Chiang, was unable to protect its cities. The Japanese Army took Beijing and Tianjin, then the trading port of Shanghai and Nanjing, the

Mao speaks with some peasants around 1937. He believed
that it was time for the peasants to rise up and break free
from the oppression of their landlords.

national capital. In late 1938, Hankou and Guiangzhou also
fell. Hundreds of thousands of Chinese were killed. The
massacre of Chinese civilians at Nanjing began in December
1937. In three months, Japanese soldiers killed two hundred
thousand civilians and raped twenty thousand women. The
Japanese commander at Nanjing, General Iwane Matsui, was
later hanged as a war criminal. By the end of 1938, Japan
controlled most of eastern China. The Chinese Army was
forced to withdraw to Sichuan Province in central China.
Japan signed anti-Communist pacts with Germany and Italy.

# World War II

China's fortunes improved when the war with Japan became part of World War II. The war began when Germany invaded Poland on September 1, 1939. Germany's dictator, Adolf Hitler, soon conquered most of Europe. In June 1940, Italy joined Germany in the war. In September, Japan signed an agreement that further allied the country with Germany and Italy. Germany invaded the Soviet Union in June 1941.

On December 7, 1941, the Japanese launched a surprise bombing attack on Pearl Harbor, a US naval base in Hawaii. Nineteen ships were sunk. Some twenty-four hundred American soldiers and sailors were killed. In response, the United States declared war on Japan. Because of these events, on December 8, China joined the Allies in World War II. The main members of the Allies were the United States, Great Britain, China, and the Soviet Union. Against them stood Germany, Italy, and Japan, known as the Axis powers.

The Chinese now had the Allies' support against Japan, which was rapidly conquering Southeast Asia and islands in the Pacific. China gained respect among the Allied countries. In 1942 Chiang became the supreme commander of the Allied forces in China. He was one of the four Allied leaders, who also included Prime Minister Winston Churchill of Great Britain, Joseph Stalin of the Soviet Union, and President Franklin D. Roosevelt of the United States. Support from the United States aided the Chinese. US major general Joseph W. Stilwell served as Chiang's chief of staff and helped to train the Chinese Army. The United States trained Chinese men as pilots and established an air force in China.

World War II ended after US president Harry Truman, who took office after Roosevelt died in 1945, ordered the dropping of atomic bombs on two Japanese cities. Bombs were dropped on Hiroshima and Nagasaki on August 6 and August 9, 1945, respectively. Over 240,000 Japanese civilians were killed in the bombings. Japan was defeated. Yet the war inflicted huge casualties on China. Some twenty million Chinese died in the fighting. Millions of Chinese starved because the Japanese took their food supplies. China's economy was in tatters. Riots and strikes disrupted the cities.

## Civil War

With the Japanese defeat, China was no longer united against a common foreign foe. Tensions rose between the

## Primary Source: Chiang Kai-shek's Speech

"In our present struggle against Japan we have been able to live up to this high principle. The hearts of our people are absolutely united. Under the guidance of the government even the old and the weak, the women and the children, are conscious of the necessity of defending themselves against the enemy...Indeed, their spirit is such that they are willing to lay down their lives without a murmur. No one will barter his national birthright for slavery to Japan.... today, China cannot be conquered."[4]

—In the midst of the bitter war with Japan, Chinese General Chiang Kai-shek gave the speech "China Cannot Be Conquered," in which he proclaimed the unity of China and the determination of its people.

Chiang Kai-shek meets with American president Franklin D. Roosevelt (center) and British prime minister Winston Churchill in 1943. Along with Russia, they represented the major Allied forces in World War II.

Communists and Kuomintang. To avert more war, Truman sent US general George C. Marshall to China to help the two sides reach a settlement. The Marshall peace talks were unsuccessful. In March 1946, an all-out civil war erupted. The Soviet Union backed the Communists, while the United States supported the Kuomintang.

During World War II, the Communist Party had grown stronger, particularly in the countryside. Many Chinese had suffered so extremely that they had lost faith in the Kuomintang. The Communists now controlled a large area in northern China, once occupied by the Japanese. But the Red Army still had fewer men and arms than the Kuomintang. Even the Soviet leader Stalin urged Mao to dissolve his army and join Chiang's government, but Mao refused.

## Chiang Flees to Taiwan

Slowly, the Red Army built up strength. More peasants rallied behind the Communists. When the Red Army seized an area, they took land belonging to landlords and gave it to poor farmers. When Kuomintang commanders surrendered, they were sometimes allowed to become officers in the Red Army. In 1947 the Communists launched offensives and began scoring victories.

By 1949 the Communists had finally defeated the Kuomintang. Chiang Kai-shek fled with some two million refugees to Taiwan, a mountainous island one hundred miles off the China coast. Taiwan had been a Japanese colony since 1895. After World War II, China was given control over the island. In 1949 Chiang took over, imposing martial law. There, he established the Republic of China. Many Taiwanese were killed during the first years of his rule. Gradually, Taiwan, which became known as Nationalist China, moved forward toward democracy and economic stability. But mainland China refused to recognize Taiwan's independence, maintaining it was a breakaway province.

The Red Army marched triumphantly into Beijing. The Communists were determined to unify China. They also had to help China recover from war. People needed to work and eat. With Mao as leader, this would not be an ordinary recovery effort.

# The People's Republic

For centuries, the Chinese people had lived under the rule of the emperors. Their resources were stolen by foreign invaders. More recently, war and tumult had torn apart their country. Mao Zedong promised to bring a new age of hope and prosperity. He wanted to unite China and put the past behind. Under his leadership, China would move into the modern age.

On ten o'clock in the morning of October 1, 1949, Mao stood at a reviewing stand on Tiananmen gate, the Gate of Heavenly Peace. The gate marks the entrance to the Forbidden City that lies in the heart of Beijing. The Forbidden City is an impressive complex of buildings, gardens, courtyards, and lakes. Built in the fifteenth century, it was the home of the emperors. Now China's emperors were gone. Bright flags and banners flapped in the breeze. Chinese air force planes flew across the sky. Crowds filled Tiananmen Square, the open plaza outside the Forbidden City. The people of China were eager to hear the voice of their new leader.

Surrounded by senior members of the Chinese Communist Party, Mao was clearly in control. Standing six feet tall, he wore a modest dark suit and simple worker's

Mao announces the formation of the People's Republic of China on October 1, 1949.

cap. Speaking into a microphone, Mao announced the formation of the People's Republic of China (PRC). China would no longer be insulted and humiliated. A new era had begun. In the square, the crowd shouted "Long Live the People's Republic of China," and slogans and revolutionary songs filled the air. Under a clear sky, a red flag with five golden stars was raised. The red symbolized the Communist revolution—and the stars represented the unity of the Chinese people. It was the new flag of the PRC.

## "The Liberation"

Many years later, Mao's personal physician, Dr. Li Zhisui, remembered that day. He had listened to Mao's words with

# Primary Source: "The Chinese People Have Stood Up!"

**From now on our nation will belong to the community of the peace-loving and freedom-loving nations of the world and work courageously and industriously to foster its own civilization and well-being and at the same time to promote world peace and freedom. Ours will no longer be a nation subject to insult and humiliation. We have stood up.[1]**

—*Mao gave this speech on September 21, 1949, during his address at the First Plenary Session of the Chinese People's Political Consultative Conference.*

great hope. "I was so full of joy my heart nearly burst out of my throat, and tears welled up in my eyes. I was so proud of China, so full of hope, so happy that the exploitation and suffering, the aggression from foreigners would be gone forever," he observed.[2]

The Chinese people called the revolution, the "liberation." Mao promised that the old lines between landlords and peasants would disappear. People would work together as equals for the common good. China would be transformed from a land of poor farmers into a modern industrialized nation. Chinese who had left during the civil war soon returned to their country.

Mao was not a young man in 1949. He was fifty-six years old. He had spent much of his youth as a revolutionary and soldier, fighting against those in power. Now he was in charge. He was about to embark on a very different and difficult challenge: leading a troubled nation of over 400 million people.

# Stalin

Mao needed support from outside China. The Cold War, or the rivalry between groups of Communist and non-Communist nations that had developed after World War II, was under way. To gain power, nations had to align with either the Soviet Union, which led the Eastern bloc of Communist nations, or the United States and its democratic allies, known as the Western bloc. The Soviets had supported the Chinese Communists for decades. Now Mao needed their help once again.

Soon after the Communist victory, Mao traveled to the Soviet Union. He met with Soviet leader Joseph Stalin to seek support. In February 1950, China and the Soviet

Union signed the Treaty of Friendship, Alliance and Mutual Assistance. The two countries pledged to come to each other's aid if attacked. Yet the treaty was not entirely equal. It gave the Soviets certain economic rights in China, such as allowing Soviet companies to exploit mineral resources in Manchuria. The treaty also gave independence to Outer Mongolia, a region that China long considered as its own. Still, the Soviet Union was China's only major ally.

## The Korean War

Soon China was swept into war again. In October 1950, Mao's army invaded its neighbor to the west, Tibet, which had an uneasy relationship with China. A Communist government led by Chinese officials was installed. Tibetans were compelled to raise red flags and Mao posters in their homes. The deeply religious people were forced to give up their Buddhist practices, and their temples were destroyed.

More trouble occurred on China's northeast coast, where the Korean peninsula extends. For more than one thousand years, the small country of Korea was unified and independent. But in the late 1800s, China, Russia, and Japan fought to control Korea. In 1910, Japan declared Korea part of the Japanese Empire. After Japan lost World War II, the Allies agreed to restore Korean independence in a cooperative manner. But relations between the Allied countries quickly deteriorated. Korea was split in half. A democratic government allied with the United States was established in the south. The Soviets backed the Communist government in the north.

Civil war broke out when North Korean troops invaded South Korea on June 25, 1950. The war became an international conflict between Communist and non-

This painting depicts the 1950 signing of the Treaty of Friendship, Alliance and Mutual Assistance between China and Russia. Mao and Stalin are pictured in the center, shaking hands.

Communist countries. Mao needed Korea as a Communist ally. On October 25, 1950, Chinese troops crossed the Yalu River into North Korea. All told, China sent more than 2.3 million troops to support North Korea. On the other side, Japan, the United States, and some twenty other countries sent arms and men to South Korea. After fierce fighting and heavy casualties on both sides, a truce that permanently divided North Korea and South Korea was signed in July 1953. Neither side could claim a victory.

The war effort helped unify China. However, it fed anti-American sentiment among the Chinese people. China was also condemned by the United Nations (UN). China had lost one million soldiers, including Mao's son, Mao Anying. Mao Anying was twenty-eight years old and a volunteer in Korea assigned to headquarters as a staff officer and Russian interpreter. On November 25, 1950, his offices were hit by a US and UN bomb, and he was killed. Mao ordered that Anying's body remain in North Korea as a symbol of his duty to China. "In war there must be sacrifice. Without sacrifice there will be no victory. There are no parents in the world who do not treasure their children," said Mao.[3]

# China Rebuilds

With the end of the Korean War, China began to rebuild its economy. Decades of war had left it in shambles. When Chiang Kai-shek fled to Taiwan, he took China's gold reserves, and many business owners followed him. Railways and shipping harbors had to be rebuilt. Trade needed to be established.

Railways, shipping companies, and other industries were now owned by the government, not by individuals. The state was the main employer. People were paid according to how much basic necessities, like rice or oil, they could buy with their salaries. To control inflation, or the rising cost of living, the government took over the banking system and regulated the trade of goods. The money and trade flow were brought under control, and inflation was reduced.

# Collective Farms

Mao also set about reforming the agricultural system. China relied on its land to feed its people, estimated at between 400 and 600 million in the 1950s. Yet no more than 15 percent of China's land is fertile. Even land suitable for planting is vulnerable to droughts and floods. The land, therefore, has to be carefully managed to yield as much food as possible.

Mao wanted to give the land to the peasants. He also wanted to change the balance of power from landlord to peasant. Starting in 1950, Mao ordered the redistribution of land and the elimination of landlords. A reign of terror began. By December 1952, the land had been seized, but only with terrible bloodshed. Landlords were shot and killed in front of crowds of peasants. The families of landlords lost everything. The peasants, for the first time, had their own small plots, but not for long.

In 1953, Mao launched China's first Five-Year Plan, using the Soviet model for development, to boost both agricultural and industrial production. "What can we make at present? We can make tables and chairs, teacups and teapots, we can grow grain and grind it into flour, and we can make paper. But we can't make a single motor car, plane, tank, or tractor," stated Mao in 1954.[4] Mao encouraged the development of iron, steel, electric power, and machinery industries. The Soviet Union sent money and advisors to help develop heavy industry. In return, China gave the Soviets its grain. This arrangement continued even when famine struck China in the late 1950s.

Mao decided that farmers would do better if they worked together in agricultural collectives. "The only way for the majority of the peasants to shake off poverty, improve their livelihood and fight natural calamities is to unite and go forward along the high road of socialism," stated Mao.[5] Families pooled their equipment and land in hopes of producing many more crops. By 1957 there were nearly 800,000 collective farms.

Mao (left) visits a collective farm in Moscow in 1950. He based his agricultural reforms on the Soviet model, placing the land in the hands of the peasants. The reforms were not successful.

## One-Party Government

A new government was put into place in Beijing to carry out the many reforms. Its basic structure has remained in place since the 1950s. China would be led by three bodies: the Communist Party, the State Council that runs the government, and the People's Liberation Army, formerly the Red Army. By 1954 Mao was head of all three. He was chairman of the Chinese Communist Party, chief of state of the People's Republic of China (PRC), and chairman of the military.

China's constitution has evolved over the years. The first constitution was adopted in 1954. The latest was passed in 1982 and amended in 1993. The current Chinese

Constitution states, "The People's Republic of China is a socialist state under the people's democratic dictatorship led by the working class and based on the alliance of workers and peasants."[6] The people do not vote for their leaders in open democratic elections, as citizens do in the United States. China is basically a one-party system of government, its leaders selected by the Communist Party.

While the Communist Party and government are separate, the party approves every decision. Elected officials are members of the party. Most important civilian, police, and military jobs are assigned to party members. In the PRC's first years, veterans of the Long March took top government positions. However, only a small percentage of the population belonged to the party. The Communist Party had a membership of roughly 4.5 million, mostly peasants, in 1949. Today, about 5 percent of Chinese, over 64.5 million, are members of the party.

Following Lenin's practice in the Soviet Union, the government and Communist Party are shaped like pyramids. A few powerful people rule at the top. The party chairman, now called the general secretary, is the leader of the party. Beneath him is the Secretariat, a small group of senior party leaders. The Secretariat has the final say in party decisions. Beneath the Secretariat is the Politburo, the party's inner power circle. The Politburo appoints workers to government, civilian, and military positions. It also establishes policy guidelines. The three-hundred-member Central Committee is under the Politburo. These leaders are elected by the National Party Congress, a larger body with close to two thousand representatives from all regions of China. The National Party Congress meets to vote on party policies and programs, but in truth has little authority. However, future party leaders often emerge from the congress.

China's state is led by a president and vice president, who also hold high positions in the Communist Party. The president nominates the premier, who is the head of the government. The premier heads the State Council, made up of representatives from ministries, commissions, and other institutions, which runs the government on a daily basis. In 1949 Zhou Enlai became China's first premier and foreign minister. He was a veteran of the Long March and a longtime party leader. More interested in improving people's lives than strictly following Mao's Communist ideals, Zhou steered Mao away from some of his more radical ideas.

The PRC's Constitution states: "all power in the People's Republic of China belongs to the people."[7] In practice, the people are represented in China's government by the National People's Congress, made up of three thousand delegates elected by local people's congresses in counties and towns across the country. The National People's Congress meets once a year to amend the constitution, enact laws, elect government officials, approve the national economic plan and budget, and make other decisions. Yet the congress usually follows orders from the Communist Party's Politburo.

China's large armed forces, which include an army, navy, and air force, are led by the Military Commission of the Communist Party and the Central Military Commission of the government. The People's Liberation Army not only defends the country, it also enforces the Communist Party's policies and programs. Many of China's military leaders have been party leaders. Mao relied on the support of the military to carry out his programs.

# Healthier Nation

Reaching out to even the smallest, most remote village, the massive government bureaucracy unified China for the first time in years. It also exerted strict control over the Chinese people. The government had many problems to tackle. One priority was public health. In the early 1950s, the average Chinese life expectancy was very low. Many children died before reaching adulthood. Mao wanted to improve the health of his people. The government set out to promote basic hygiene, preventive health care, and family planning.

In the past, many Chinese did not have access to medical care. A system of universal access to medical treatment and free preventive care was put into place. Improving the health of rural workers was a priority for Mao. Under his leadership, nearly the entire rural population was provided with virtually free basic health care services. Doctors were sent to the countryside. Clinics and pharmacies were set up even in remote villages.

Mass campaigns were started to fight contagious diseases. Campaigns to vaccinate people helped to nearly wipe out deadly diseases such as cholera, typhoid, and scarlet fever. The incidence of other infectious and parasitic diseases was reduced. Tuberculosis, a major health hazard in 1949, remained a problem to some extent into the 1980s, as did other diseases such as hepatitis, malaria, and dysentery.

Outside the large cities, most of China had no modern sewage system. In rural areas, human waste had always been collected and scattered in the fields as fertilizer. This led to the spread of parasites and disease. To combat this problem, people were ordered to build facilities to treat human waste. Peasants began treating human waste in composting and storage pits, and with chemicals. They were ordered to dig deep wells to access cleaner water. As a result of these and other campaigns, health standards rapidly improved.

## Learning to Read

Along with improving health, Mao wanted his people educated. Prior to 1949, most peasants could not read. Few peasants were able to take the time away from the fields to learn the thousands of Chinese characters necessary to read and write. Mao wanted every child to have a basic education.

The education system was brought under the central government. New schools were built. Attendance at primary schools rose from twenty-four million in 1949 to sixty-four million in 1957. More students attended middle schools, technical schools, and universities, as well. By 1985 about 96 percent of school-age children were enrolled in some 832,300 primary schools. Still, many families could not pay the school fees. Children dropped out early. More boys than girls attended school. Thus, more women remained unable to read or write.

## Half the Sky

Overall, however, the status of women did improve under Mao. Chinese culture was traditionally centered around men. In ancient China, girls had no names until they married and took their husband's surname. After marriage, the bride joined her husband's family, where she was considered inferior to her mother-in-law and her husband.

Mao liked to say that women hold up half the sky. He outlawed child marriages and arranged marriages, the sale of brides, wife beating, and prostitution. The 1950 Marriage

**Children attend a school that was set up by the Communists. One of the goals of Mao's reforms was to educate the Chinese people.**

Law did away with the second-class legal status of women. Women could own property and choose their husbands, rather than submit to arranged marriages. They were given equal rights over property and divorce settlements. Girls could attend school, and women worked alongside men in the fields or factories. "In order to build a great socialist society, it is of the utmost importance to arouse the broad masses of women to join in productive activity. Men and women must receive equal pay for equal work in production," Mao wrote.[8]

Women were encouraged to become managers and party officials. Yet women rarely became leaders. With few exceptions, men held the important positions in the party and the government. Women were still responsible for the children and housework. Most women worked while pregnant. Still, families preferred sons, who would carry on the family name.

# Religion

The Communist Party regarded religion as a threat to the state's authority and a diversion from more important matters. Many Chinese followed the Buddhist or Taoist religions. Some Chinese converted to Christianity under the influence of European missionaries. Others lived according to the teachings of Confucius and ancestor worship, or combined more than one religion. The Communists expected that religious beliefs would just fade away as people became educated and understood the world from a more scientific viewpoint, but meanwhile religion was restricted in the PRC.

The government forbade public religious festivals. During China's land reform in the 1950s, monasteries and temples lost their lands and buildings. Buddhist monks were forced to do nonreligious work. Chinese Protestants and Roman Catholics had to defend their loyalty to the state and party. Catholics, who revered their leader, the pope, were persecuted. The Chinese Catholic Church broke away from the pope in order to show its loyalty to the government.

# Disloyalty

People were denied other personal liberties as well. After all, Mao was determined to change society. The individual was less important than the state. During the 1950s, Mao launched the Four Olds campaign to wipe out old ideas, habits, customs and cultures. Another campaign, known as the Three Anti's, was aimed at eliminating waste and corruption in government. The Five Anti's campaign was directed at business owners and wealthy people, to stop bribery, tax fraud, and other cheating. These campaigns aimed to modify people's behavior to benefit the state.

People were not allowed to criticize the government or to question the Communist Party. Chinese art, literature, and music had to serve the revolution. Artists and writers were attacked if their work did not appear patriotic. Newspapers and radio broadcasts were carefully checked for anti-Communist sentiment. Even the party newspaper, *The People's Daily*, was checked for disloyalty. Mao fired the editor for not backing the new government.

Critics of the government were called counter-revolutionaries. They were severely punished. Hundreds of thousands of these people were killed during the PRC's early years, although the exact number is uncertain. Others had to undergo thought reform. People were sent to prison and labor camps for reeducation. Reeducation was a method of imposing Communist Party ideas on the people. As China's leader, Mao was following the strong-arm philosophy of legalism. The will of Mao and the Communist Party were not to be challenged.

## Loss of Freedom

Under Mao, the lives of the Chinese people changed in many ways. People were assigned where to live and what work to do. They needed permission to marry and, later, to have children. This system seemed to offer a great security net. However, in exchange for the promise of security, the people of China lost many personal freedoms. It did not take long for the optimism that swept through China in 1949 to be replaced with a more complicated reality.

# CHAPTER 7

# Drought and Famine

By the late 1950's, the Chinese had not seen great advancements or improvements in their lives. Still hungry, they were impatient. Mao needed a different tactic to harness his people's support for the Communist revolution. But a revolution can take time, as Mao was observing. He needed the people to be patient. Perhaps a show of humility on the part of China's leader might reignite their enthusiasm. Mao decided to open his ears to people's criticisms and concerns. In a speech in February 1957, Mao spoke about how revolutions take time, but struggle must go on. Then he stepped back and, for a passing moment, let the Chinese people have a voice.

## The People Speak

For a brief period in 1957, Mao allowed criticism of his government. He decided that limited debates among the masses were helpful. Perhaps more art, literature, and science would be good for China, he thought. Fresh ideas might improve and unify China. Long suspicious of intellectuals and artists, Mao now hoped to win their support.

Despite Mao's efforts to improve the peasants' lot during the 1950s, many were still going hungry.

Mao suggested that people voice their honest opinions of the government. He persuaded his colleagues to allow intellectuals and nonparty members to criticize the party. To launch the campaign, he used this quote from classical Chinese poetry, "Let a hundred flowers bloom, and let a hundred schools of thought contend."[1] He meant that many ideas and opinions could flourish together.

At first, people were fearful of speaking out. In the past, critics had been severely punished. They remembered the campaign against enemies of the state in the early 1950s. Yet by the summer of 1957, people began openly expressing their views. People complained about the government, Marxism, and restrictions on their creative work. Criticisms were posted on public walls and published in national newspapers.

Mao and other officials were surprised by the flood of complaints and accusations. After only a few weeks, Mao brutally retaliated. The critics were labeled "rightists" and enemies of the people and forced to take back what they had said or written. By the fall of 1957, the Anti-Rightist Campaign had silenced Mao's critics. Hundreds of thousands of people lost their jobs, were imprisoned, or were sent to the countryside to do hard labor. Their absence left a huge void. "The cost to China's scientific and economic establishment was as high as it was to the creative arts, literature, and education generally," wrote historian Jonathan Spence.[2] The window of free speech closed as suddenly as it had opened in China.

## Great Leap Forward

Hoping to move the economy forward, Mao launched the second Five-Year Plan in 1957 to improve production in both agriculture and industry. The government also began reforming education to stress science and engineering. Mao wanted China to catch up with industrialized nations, like Great Britain. He wanted major changes in Chinese society, as well.

In February 1958, the National People's Congress announced the start of the Great Leap Forward. The PRC reorganized rural farmland into People's Communes. Private property was abolished. The state now owned the land and everyone worked together. In the communes, people shared their tools, labor, animals, and land, and farmed the land together, pooling profits. The communes replaced the family unit and the village support system. People gave up their homes and property. Soon, most of China's farmland was divided into communes, each made up of between two thousand and twenty thousand households.

Each commune had its own government and economy. The communes were divided into production brigades and production teams. Men and women worked in the fields, while children were cared for in communal nurseries and attended communal schools. Everyone ate together in communal kitchens. "One village, one stove. Everyone had to eat in the canteen," recalled Wang Jiufu a village party chief in Yan'an.[3] The adults lived in dormitories. Often, the women lived separately from the men.

To further boost the economy, people were ordered to build massive public works projects. Over 100 million people were put to work. They constructed irrigation systems to bring water to farmland. They dug reservoirs to provide water for villages. They built dams. As a result of these huge projects, fields were deserted and the usual labor went neglected.

The Great Leap also called for increases in steel, electricity, and coal production. Mao ordered people in the countryside to build steel furnaces. They were told to melt pots and pans and even rocks that might contain iron ore. Millions of small furnaces were built in the backyards of homes and businesses. The nation's coal went to the furnaces, leaving trains without fuel. But the metal created in backyard furnaces was full of impurities and was therefore useless. "We cooked the rocks day and night for a year and couldn't make one . . . piece of steel!" said Wang Jiufu.[4]

Peasants were urged to assault the "four pests"—rats, sparrows, flies, and mosquitoes—and snails that transmit a serious disease. Children were told to catch flies, which they brought to party officials to be counted. However, the cure was often worse than the problem. By killing the sparrows that eat insects, people were unintentionally allowing flies and mosquitos to multiply.

## Terrible Famine

Despite the labor of millions, the Great Leap Forward was a disaster. Agricultural production increased at first, but fertile land had been lost. The remaining farmland was overused. Crops began to fail. Local commune officials competed against each other. They overestimated their farm production figures. The Communist Party then taxed the communes based on the inaccurate figures. Taxes were collected in grain, not money, reducing the amount of grain available for food. People were going hungry.

Mao refused to see what was happening. After traveling around the country, the leader praised the progress he thought he saw. In an interview with a reporter on September 29, 1958, Mao declared, "During this trip, I have witnessed the tremendous energy of the masses. On this foundation it is possible to accomplish any task whatsoever."[5] He urged the people to work even harder, and to become even more dedicated to the revolution. To Mao, the transformation of the countryside was a success.

The party leaders were frightened to tell Mao that the Chinese people were starving. To make matters even worse, the country was plagued by severe weather. In 1959 droughts in some parts of China, and flash floods in other regions, brought devastating crop failures. A terrible famine swept through China. By 1962, as many as thirty million people were dead of starvation.

# Loss of Soviets

Mao was also facing the breakdown in China's relationship with its important ally, the Soviet Union. After Joseph Stalin's death in 1953, Nikita Khrushchev became the leader of the Soviet Union. Stalin had not always supported the Chinese Communists, particularly before 1949. Nevertheless, Mao was angered when Khrushchev turned on Stalin and his programs. In a speech he gave in February 1956, Khrushchev called Stalin a murderer and accused the former leader of tyranny and terror. As a result, Mao feared that one day his people might reject him also.

The two countries had other conflicts as well. The Chinese government worried that the Soviets' nuclear weapons program could threaten China's interests. Also, Khrushchev was critical of many of Mao's economic and social policies. In a serious blow to China, the Soviet Union withdrew its financial aid and advisers in 1960. Without Soviet support, China's recovery from the famine of the late 1950s would be made much more difficult.

In 1958 Mao visited farmers in Zhejiang to congratulate them on their production numbers. In reality, these numbers were inflated and the country's agricultural system was in dire straits.

# Mao Steps Back

In the summer of 1959, party leaders met at Lushan to talk about the Great Leap Forward. The minister of defense, Peng Dehuai, criticized Mao for the economic disaster. He believed China needed Soviet support, and was upset that the ties had been broken. Angry at the criticism, Mao expelled Peng and his followers from the government. He appointed Lin Biao, a Mao loyalist, as the new defense minister.

Peng was not the only person who thought Mao had made mistakes. Two party leaders, Deng Xiaoping and Liu Shoaqi, were preparing to replace Mao and his radical ideas. Deng was a founder of the Red Army and secretary general of the Communist Party since 1954. Liu was the vice president of the People's Republic and second to Mao in leadership. They wanted to concentrate less on political ideas; they instead wanted to build the economy and feed the people. "They treated me like a dead ancestor," he said of Deng and Liu.[6] Mao had little choice but to give up his power, at least in part. In the spring of 1959, he stepped down as president of the PRC. He remained chairman of the Chinese Communist Party. Liu replaced him as leader of the government.

In the next years, Deng worked with Liu and Zhou Enlai, China's premier, to help China recover and restore the people's confidence. Peasants had supported the revolution because it promised them a better life. Under Communism, however, no matter how hard they worked, they earned neither more nor less than anyone else. Families wanted their own homes and plots of land. In response, Deng and his colleagues abolished the communes and the backyard furnaces. They returned property to the people. They began to pay workers to produce consumer goods. To revive the economy, the leaders initiated emergency measures such as importing grain from the West. These practical steps were successful. By the mid-1960s, food supplies were back to normal.

Although the economic crisis was over, China would see more dark years under Mao. During the next decade, Mao would take desperate measures to restore his authority. Many Chinese people would suffer terrible losses in Mao's new bid for power.

# "The East Is Red"

Tiananmen Square in Beijing was a noisy sea of red and green on August 18, 1966. Hundreds of thousands of young people, wearing red armbands on their green military uniforms, chanted revolutionary slogans. They were members of the Red Guard, a mostly teenage army that was full of energy and passion. Mao Zedong was also there that day. He stood next to his army leader, Lin Biao, in front of the crowds. He wore an army uniform and a red star on his cap. In a gesture that would go down in history, a young woman presented Mao with a Red Guard armband. He was now one of them. Together, Mao and the Red Guards would spread terror and chaos across China. But for now, optimism and jubilation filled the square. As one writer described it: "Many of the students, overcome with emotion, began sobbing with joy."[1]

## Destroy the Traditions

By the mid-1960s, Mao was frustrated that his revolution was moving too slowly. The ideas and culture of Chinese life for so many centuries had not fallen away quickly enough for his satisfaction. He was afraid that people were not standing

A young woman gives Mao the armband of the Red Guard during a celebration of the Cultural Revolution on August 18, 1966.

behind his ideas about Communism and a new China. Mao believed that the old ways blocked progress. If he did not act decisively to banish them once and for all, the Communist revolution might fail.

Mao was also uneasy about his comrades. He suspected they were not fully devoted to the revolution and that decisions were being made without him. He wondered if he still had their respect and loyalty. The moderate leaders of the Communist Party were steering China away from his vision, Mao believed. He was especially suspicious of educated people, or intellectuals. He feared that they threatened his authority.

The solution, Mao decided, was to stir up conflict again. He called the new upheaval the Great Proletarian Cultural Revolution. It is now known as the Cultural Revolution. With the strong arm of the People's Liberation Army and the enthusiasm of young Red Guards, Mao set out to destroy his enemies and all that was traditional in China.

This revolution wasn't fought on mountaintops or distant villages. It was fought in the heart of China's villages and cities—and the enemies were the old thoughts and traditions. The soldiers were China's young people. Mao relied on young people to carry out his new revolution. They were to turn against their own parents and grandparents, their teachers and village leaders. They were to turn against all that was old.

## Four Olds

Mao was determined to destroy the Four Olds—the old ideas, old customs, old culture, and old habits. According to Mao, the bourgeoisie, or middle class, was using the Four Olds to corrupt the masses and capture their minds. He called on the masses to lead his newest battle. "Trust the masses, rely on them, and respect their initiative, cast out fear and don't be afraid of disturbances," he said.[2]

Many people in the crowd waved a small red book, *Quotations from Chairman Mao Tse-tung*. Better known as *The Little Red Book*, it was compiled by Lin in the early 1960s and published in 1966. The pages contained hundreds of excerpts from Mao's writings and speeches. The book's slogans would be memorized by millions of Chinese.

## The Red Guards

Mao turned to young people to lead his new revolution. Schools were closed. Students put away their books to form Red Guard units. Teenagers flooded into Beijing to join the Red Guards, and more huge rallies were held in Tiananmen Square. Mao opened the railroads to free passage. Red Guards from Beijing traveled in squads to spread the Cultural Revolution to the rest of China.

The Red Guards followed the "four big rights"—the right to speak out freely, air views fully, hold great debates, and write "big character posters." They wrote criticisms of people on the huge posters, which were hung on public walls for everyone to see. Everything changed, even the names of streets and businesses. In Changsha, for example, a park was renamed "People's Park" and a shop hung out a new sign: "The East Is Red Food Store." "All this was extremely confusing, especially for the old people, and everybody was always getting off at the wrong bus stop and getting lost," Liang Heng describes in his memoir, *Son of the Revolution*.[3] Even babies were given revolutionary names.

The traditional respect for the hierarchy of society, a part of the Confucian value system, disappeared. Children were told to turn on their parents for their old thoughts and customs. They forced their grandparents out to sweep the streets. Students criticized their teachers. Even doctors, held in deep regard in China, were denounced and humiliated.

Millions were caught up in the frenzy. As in other countries in the 1960s, the young people were rebelling against traditions. In addition, many of them loved and idolized Mao. They were willing to do anything for his approval. Jung Chang, in her memoir *Wild Swans*, describes her excitement at joining the Red Guards. She was proud of her Red Guard armband with its gold characters. "I was not forced to join the Red Guards. I was keen to do so . . . it never occurred to me to question the Cultural Revolution or the Red Guards . . . They were Mao's creations, and Mao was beyond contemplation," she recalled.[4]

## Violence Reigns

Encouraged by Mao, the Red Guards launched a campaign of destruction. "Mao had found his new guerrilla army to assault the political heights. A whole generation of young Chinese was ready to die, and to kill, for him, with unquestioning obedience. And kill they did," wrote Mao biographer Philip Short.[5] The police supplied the Red Guards with names of people who were enemies of the party. The Red Guards tore apart their homes, searching for objects that they felt represented old culture.

People accused of being rightists, landlords, rich peasants, or traitors faced humiliation or much worse. Sometimes they had to walk through the streets wearing tall dunce caps. Some were killed. Others were sent to the countryside to do hard labor. "The number of victims from the uncoordinated violence of the Cultural Revolution is incalculable, but there were many millions," wrote historian Jonathan Spence.[6]

Professionals such as teachers and writers were considered threats to the revolution. Lao She, author of a best-selling book, *Rickshaw Boy*, was seized by the Red Guards. He was taken to the courtyard of a public building in Beijing. There, he and other writers and artists were given yin-yang haircuts—meaning only half their heads were shaved. Black ink was poured over their faces. The Red Guards beat them violently, then sent them home. Like many victims during that time, Lao She, at sixty-seven, could not endure the shame. The following day, he drowned himself in a local lake.

## "Self-Criticism"

The targets of the Red Guards often had to attend "struggle meetings" in large community buildings or arenas. They were forced to stand on public platforms and read a "self-criticism," or confession. The crowd heckled and jeered the victim, even a friend, relative, or neighbor. The victims often collapsed on stage or were beaten by the crowd. The purpose was to exhaust and humiliate the victims, both physically and mentally.

Some victims lived to tell their story. Nien Cheng was the widow of an official of Chiang Kai-shek's government and an employee of Shell Oil. In August 1966, Red Guards arrested her for being a spy. She was imprisoned in solitary confinement for more than six years. During that time, she underwent interrogation and struggle meetings. In her memoir, *Life and Death in Shanghai*, Cheng describes a struggle meeting: "[T]he audience jumped up from their seats when the speaker told them I was a spy for the

During the Cultural Revolution, children and adults were encouraged to read *Quotations from Chairman Mao Tse-Tung*, also known as *The Little Red Book*. The Red Guards read from the book each morning before starting their day.

imperialists. They expressed their anger and indignation by crowding around me to shout abuse," she recalls.[7] She was forced to stand in the jet position, with her hands raised painfully, while her head was bowed. Having done nothing wrong, Cheng refused to confess she was an enemy of the state.

## Burning Books

Mao considered China's cultural treasures to be obstacles to progress. Although he was a poet and his study was filled with books, he encouraged the destruction of literature. The Red Guards burned books in public bonfires. Music and art were also destroyed. The Red Guards smashed musical instruments. They raided the opera house and museums in Beijing, destroying costumes, stage props, swords, and priceless objects.

The Communists had always been wary of organized religion and its sway on the population. Now they took sledgehammers to the shrines of Confucius. Red Guards burned Buddhist temples and hacked down statues honoring family ancestors.

Red Guards arrived in Tibet in July 1966. In 1959 a failed uprising against Chinese rule had left tens of thousands of Tibetans dead and led to the exile of the Tibetan spiritual leader, the Dalai Lama, to India. The Red Guards enlisted young Tibetans in the Cultural Revolution. From 1966 to 1969, the young rebels destroyed monasteries, temples, and other holy sites. It was not until the 1980s that monasteries were allowed to open and religious life resumed in Tibet. Tibet was still under Chinese rule in 2003, and an international Free Tibet movement continued.

Also during the 1960s, the government sent young revolutionaries to rural areas to dispense medical care. The "barefoot doctors" lived in villages and provided basic medical care. They carried their medical kits over their shoulders. When they were not working in medicine, they toiled with the peasants in the rice paddies. By the early 1970s, there were almost two million barefoot doctors. While they improved health care, they also helped increase the wide reach of the Communist state.

## The Cult of Mao

In the cities of China, loudspeakers awoke people at dawn with the song, "The East Is Red." The tune was from an

# Primary Source: "Sailing the Sea Depends on the Helmsman"

A helmsman is needed for sailing in the ocean.
The sun is needed for all things to grow.
Plants grow stronger when nourished by morning dew.
Mao Zedong's Thought is needed for the revolutionary cause.
Fish cannot live without water.
Melon cannot grow without vines.
The revolutionary masses cannot survive without the
     Communist Party.
Mao Zedong's Thought is the forever shining sun.[8]

*—This song, which was popular during the Cultural Revolution, was sung by the Red Guards at the end of rallies and events.*

old Chinese folk song. The lyrics were rewritten to glorify Mao and the Communist revolution. Like most of the music promoted by the PRC, the song was propaganda. It was sung to arouse enthusiasm for the revolution and devotion to Mao.

Mao's picture hung on buildings, in public squares, and in private homes. People greeted each other with praises to Mao and carried copies of *The Little Red Book*. When couples got married, they did so in front of his portrait. In schools that remained open, students started the day by bowing to his portrait. They studied Mao's thought and recited pledges of loyalty like this one: "A long, long life to Chairman Mao. Chairman Mao, you are the red sun in our hearts. We are sun flowers. Sun flowers always face the red sun. We think of you day and night. We wish you a long life."[9]

By the late 1960s, Mao had become like a Chinese emperor. While his revolution was for the masses, Mao lived in relative luxury in his elegant quarters in the Forbidden City in Beijing. He swam in his private swimming pool. He traveled in a private train, rarely mingling with the Chinese people. People quickly agreed with him, mostly out of fear. "Mao was a dictator. There were no other preferences but his. Those of us around him had to grant his every wish. To assert one's individuality in Mao's imperial court would have been an invitation to disaster," wrote Dr. Li Zhisui, Mao's doctor.[10]

Yet Mao still seemed insecure. Fearful of betrayals, he fired his secretaries and aides. Some were sent to prison. Mao accused old comrades of pushing China toward capitalism and undermining the revolution. No one, it seemed, was safe from Mao's attacks.

## Expelling Leaders

Pu Yi, the emperor who had been expelled in 1924, was persecuted during the Cultural Revolution. He later worked as a gardener and died in 1967, marking the end of a dynasty that had fallen long before.

Mao set out to restore his authority by going after moderate party leaders. He accused them of taking the so-called capitalist road. Deng Xiaoping, general secretary of the Communist Party, was denounced for promoting capitalism. In October 1969, Deng, who had survived the Long March, was exiled to Nanchang, in Jiangxi Province, where he was heavily guarded. He worked as a laborer in a tractor plant.

# Primary Source: Mao on Revolution

**A revolution is not a dinner party, or writing an essay, or painting a picture, or doing embroidery; it cannot be so refined, so leisurely and gentle, so temperate, kind, courteous, restrained and magnanimous. A revolution is an insurrection, an act of violence by which one class overthrows another.**

*—One of the most famous of Mao's speeches and writings collected in The Little Red Book. It was originally in Mao's "Report on an Investigation of the Peasant Movement in Hunan" written in 1927.[11]*

Another important official, Liu Shaoqi, named head of state in 1959 and Mao's chosen successor, suffered even more. He was expelled from the Communist Party and stripped of his government posts. Like the lives of many party leaders, his life was destroyed. Abandoned by his old friends, he saw his children join the Red Guards. Liu was forced to admit to many "crimes" against Communism. Without medical treatment, he died in 1969 of pneumonia in a provincial prison.

## "Dragon Lady"

Mao's fourth wife, Jiang Qing, became increasingly influential. In 1937 she joined the Communists in Yan'an, after which she met and married Mao. Jiang's views were even more extreme than Mao's. Known as Madame Mao, she was willing to do anything to stay in power. She turned her attention to China's cultural heritage as a tool for the revolution.

Elaborate and colorful operas have a popular tradition in China. Jiang decided to revolutionize the Beijing Opera by replacing the traditional operas with works emphasizing Mao's doctrine. She banned all cultural expressions except six revolutionary operas. The works expressed the themes of the Cultural Revolution, such as struggle, criticism, and rehabilitation.

People flocked to see the operas. In her memoir, *Red Azalea*, writer Anchee Min describes her love of the operas as a girl:

> I became an opera fan . . . It was a proletarian statement. The revolutionary operas created by Madam Mao, Comrade Jiang Ching. To love or not love the operas was a serious political attitude. It meant to be or not to be a revolutionary.[12]

The operas did stir up patriotism. Jiang and her closest allies, Zhang Chunqiao, Yao Wenyuan, and Wang Hongwen, gained power. They became known as the Gang of Four. Along with Lin Biao, the defense minister, they held great influence on Mao.

Jiang was ruthless. She attacked anyone who she felt posed a threat to her or Mao's power. A *Time* magazine reporter described her as "the fire-breathing dragon lady of the Cultural Revolution."[13]

# A Lost Generation

China had fallen into civil disorder. People could not buy basic goods like sugar, salt, and soap. Even those who had

Mao stands with his fourth wife, Jiang Qing, who had a great deal of influence over her husband.

initially supported Mao's new revolution were dismayed. "All the things I loved were disappearing. The saddest thing of all for me was the ransacking of the library: the golden tiled roof, the delicately sculpted windows . . . Bookshelves were turned upside down . . ."[14] wrote Jung Chang, a former member of the Red Guard. Her father, a loyal Communist official, was beaten and put in detention after he refused to work with a local official. "Human anguish did not concern Mao," wrote Chang.[15]

Even Mao could no longer ignore the upheaval. Factions of the Red Guards were fighting each other. The military was getting involved. The violence was threatening to throw the country into anarchy, or civil chaos. To regain control, in July 1968, Mao disbanded the Red Guards. Some ten million Red Guards were sent to work as peasants, cleaning latrines and working the fields in rural villages.

The Cultural Revolution ended in April 1969 with the meeting of the Ninth Communist Party Congress. Mao reclaimed the party leadership. A new party constitution was passed, which stressed Mao's thought and class struggle. In 1970 Mao became supreme commander of the nation and the army. He was securely the leader of China once more.

After the Red Guards disbanded, China remained in the grips of chaos. The Gang of Four exerted control until 1976. Production had fallen in most industries. Millions had lost their homes, possessions, and jobs. The young people of this era became known as the "lost generation." They had spent their youths inciting violence or fleeing from it. They lacked the education or job training to build their futures because many had left school to join the Red Guard. The state of the "lost generation" would lead to problems in the years to come.

# Raising the
# Bamboo Curtain

In April 1972, a plane landed at Andrews Air Force Base in Maryland with a special gift from the Chinese government to the United States. Two eighteen-month-old giant pandas named Ling-Ling and Hsing-Hsing were on their way to the National Zoo. The animals' arrival captured newspaper headlines. Crowds flocked to the zoo in Washington, DC, to see the giant pandas, an endangered species that lives in vanishing bamboo forests in the mountains of China. The giant pandas were an important symbol of friendship and signaled a thawing relationship between China and the United States.

One of Mao's final achievements was to open the doors of diplomacy to the United States and the West. During most of his life, Mao had rejected the outside world. He had returned China to the isolation of its imperial past. He took only two trips outside China, both to the Soviet Union.

Yet times had changed. By the 1970s, Mao needed a strong ally to help shield against the Soviet Union's aggression and growing nuclear capabilities. Richard M. Nixon, the US president from 1969 to 1974, wanted to build relations

Giant pandas Ling-Ling and Hsing-Hsing, a gift to the United States from China in 1972, play in their yard at the National Zoo in Washington, DC. The gift arrived after President Nixon's visit to China earlier that year.

with China. He considered China an important player in the balance of world power. "Mainland China, outside the world community, completely isolated, with its leaders not in communication with world leaders, would be a danger to the whole world . . . So consequently, this step must be taken now," said Nixon in July 1971.[1]

# War in Vietnam

Building bridges would take delicate political maneuvering. The United States and China had been enemies since the Korean War. Their relationship worsened during the Vietnam conflict. The small southeast Asian nation, divided between north and south, was embroiled in the Vietnam War from 1957 to 1975. China supported Communist North Vietnam against South Vietnam and the United States. As many as fifty thousand Chinese soldiers were killed in North Vietnam.

Both China and the United States wanted to find a way to end the conflict in Vietnam. President Nixon thought that friendship with China would help reduce Soviet influence and force the Soviets to agree to limit nuclear weapons. The two countries made overtures to each other in the late 1960s and early 1970s. For example, Nixon stated publicly that he wanted to visit China. "If there is anything I want to do before I die, it is to go to China," Nixon told *Time* magazine in 1970.[2] The question was how to make the visit a reality. The two leaders got help from an unexpected corner, the sport of table tennis.

## Ping-Pong Diplomacy

Table tennis, known also as Ping-Pong, was probably introduced to China by British Army officers at the turn of the twentieth century. During the 1950s, Mao's government encouraged it as a national sport in which Chinese athletes could excel at the international level. China's effort to build national pride through table tennis was a huge success. Chinese players have won more gold and silver medals at the Summer Olympics than players from any other nation: Chinese men and women won four gold medals in table tennis events at the 2012 Summer Olympics. Table tennis is also a popular sport among ordinary Chinese young people.

In the early 1970s, table tennis formed a diplomatic bridge. Chinese and American teams attended the thirty-first World Table Tennis Championship in Japan in April 1971. The Americans were invited to play in China following the tournament. The players were the first Americans allowed into China for a cultural exchange since the Communist takeover in 1949. During their historic visit, the players performed exhibition matches. They also saw a little of

American table tennis players visit the Great Wall of China in 1971. This was the first time Americans were allowed into China for a cultural exchange since 1949.

China, which had been off-limits to the West. The athletes visited the Great Wall of China, met with Chinese students and factory workers, and attended the Canton Ballet.

Premier Zhou Enlai hosted a banquet for the Americans in the Great Hall of the People in Beijing. "You have opened a new chapter in the relations of the American and Chinese people," he declared. "I am confident that this beginning again of our friendship will certainly meet with majority support of our two peoples."[3] The United States announced it planned to remove a two-decades-long embargo, or ban, on trade with China. Not long afterward, the Chinese table-tennis team visited the United States.

# Historic Meeting

The United States and China saw an opportunity for a new relationship. In July 1971, Zhou Enlai met secretly in Beijing with Henry A. Kissinger, assistant to the president for national security affairs. Their talks laid the groundwork for a meeting between Nixon and Mao. Then in August 1971, Taiwan's seat in the United Nations was given to mainland China. This was a historic move since it meant that the United Nations no longer recognized Taiwan as an independent nation. The fact that the United States did not object to this was an encouraging sign to the People's Republic.

On February 21, 1972, President Nixon and his wife, Patricia, arrived on the presidential airplane, Air Force One, at Beijing Airport. Nixon stepped down from the plane and shook hands with Zhou. Nixon was accompanied by Kissinger, US secretary of state William Rogers, and other American officials. That same day, Nixon and Kissinger met with Mao and Zhou in Mao's private study in Zhongnanhai, his quarters in the Forbidden City.

The conversation between the two world leaders was informal. They sat in armchairs in a half circle in the room where books spilled from the bookcases. Mao did not appear healthy; his speech had been affected by a heart attack in the spring of 1971. He needed two people to help him get up from his armchair. He shuffled when he walked. Still, Mao made a few jokes to put Nixon at ease. He made a strong impression. Kissinger later wrote that the Chinese leader lived "in a style as remote and exalted as any of the emperors."[4]

The meeting signaled that the longtime foes were willing to find common ground. In Shanghai, Zhou and Nixon signed the Joint Communique of the People's Republic of China and the United States of America, an important step toward normalizing relations and reducing tensions in Asia. The communique stated that the leaders agreed to broaden understanding between the two countries. Nixon's visit paved the way for future US presidents to work with China. In 1979 the United States established diplomatic relations with China.

Nixon's China trip gave the world a glimpse of a country long hidden behind the "bamboo curtain" of Communism. (Bamboo is a type of woody grass that is common in China.) Millions of people read journalists' accounts of the Nixons attending a Beijing Opera with Mao's wife, Jiang. The Nixons also walked along the Great Wall of China. "A people that can build a wall like this certainly have a great past to be proud of, and a people who have this kind of a past must also have a great future," commented Nixon to a reporter.[5] In a gesture of friendship, the Chinese sent the United States the giant pandas, Ling-Ling and Hsing-Hsing. Mao's

**Chairman Mao shakes hands with President Nixon during his 1972 visit to China. The visit marked the end of a twenty-year ban on American trade with China.**

gift shortly after the historic visit was reciprocated by a gift from Nixon—a pair of musk oxen.

## Turmoil at the Top

China's international status had improved, but its leadership was in turmoil. Mao had failed to regain his authority, and power struggles raged over his successor. Prior to Nixon's visit, in mid-1971, Mao lost a close supporter. Lin Biao, the loyal army commander, was officially in line to be Mao's successor. After some of his generals were accused of violating party unity, Lin realized that Mao had lost confidence in him. His political future was ruined. While historians are not certain exactly what happened, Lin and other army members may have devised a plan to assassinate Mao by blowing up his train. Then Lin presumably planned to take over the government.

The plot was apparently discovered. Lin and his family fled from China in an air force plane. The plane crashed in Mongolia in September 1971, and everyone onboard was killed. In retribution for Lin's betrayal and flight from China, Mao reduced the power of the army. China now had no one in line to succeed Mao.

Mao's health was declining. Even during his meeting with Nixon, he was visibly not well. He needed constant assistance to carry out his daily activities. Gradually he was not able to walk, write, or even eat on his own.

The men who had built the PRC were aging. Zhou Enlai, premier of China since 1949, died of cancer in January 1976. Deeply admired by the Chinese people, Zhou was a voice of restraint during Mao's reign. The people of China loved and respected Zhou, but the government forbade the public mourning of his death.

The Qing Ming Festival, on April 5, is a traditional day in China for remembering the dead. On April 4, 1976, crowds of people gathered at the Revolutionary Martyr's Memorial in Tiananmen Square to lay wreaths and poems for Zhou. After the government closed the square, angry throngs broke through the barriers. The government stepped in, arresting and possibly killing some demonstrators. Two days later, former Red Guards and workers demonstrated in Tiananmen Square. They demanded an end to the Cultural

Revolution and the Gang of Four. It was the first show of public rebellion since the Communists took over China.

# Mao's Death

Mao was last seen in public on May 1, 1976, a day to honor the revolution. For a few moments, he sat overlooking Tiananmen Square and watched a display of fireworks. He suffered three heart attacks in the next few months. After drifting into a coma, he died on September 9, 1976, surrounded by members of the politburo and Dr. Li. Mao was eighty-two years old.

The news of Mao's death traveled quickly. "Funeral music followed today's announcement broadcast over the Peking radio, and 2,000 people gathered in the vast Tiananmen Square, many wearing black armbands, some weeping. Flags fluttered at half staff," wrote a *Reuters* reporter who was in Beijing that day. The announcement made over a loudspeaker proclaimed, "All victories of the Chinese people were achieved under the leadership of Chairman Mao."[6] Funeral music was played on the radio for days.

Writer Anchee Min recalled her feelings at the time. "The reddest sun dropped from the sky of the Middle Kingdom," she wrote. Like millions of others, she wore white paper flowers in her braids in mourning. "Overnight the country became an ocean of white paper flowers. Mourners beat their heads against the door, on grocery-store counters and on walls. Devastating grief," she wrote.[7]

Now, China had to find its way after the death of Mao Zedong.

# China After Mao

**M**any decades after his death, Mao still holds a position of honor in China. His enormous portrait hangs on the outer wall of the Mao Zedong Memorial Hall in Tiananmen Square in Beijing. Tourists line up to view Mao's corpse inside the hall, and then pose for a photo under the portrait. All over China, similar portraits of Mao are visible. His face is on paper currency as well. Many Chinese still consider Mao a towering figure who deserves respect, if not adulation. "Rich and poor, young and old, many mainlanders continue to look to him as a spiritual leader who stood up to foreign imperial powers and ended a century of humiliation," wrote Verna Yu in the *South China Morning Post* in 2013.[1] But today's China has also chosen to move beyond Mao in many ways—a journey that is still unfolding.

## A New Era

After leading China from 1949 until 1976, Mao's death left China without a map to chart its future. The upheaval of the Cultural Revolution continued to fester. Mao's dream of a Communist revolution had not been fully achieved. Poverty

Today a giant portrait of Mao still adorns the Gate of Heavenly Peace at Tiananmen in Beijing. The portrait is replaced with a new one every year.

was rampant. "Mao left a severely damaged and backward China," wrote Andrew G. Walder in *China Under Mao*.[2] Without a willingness to change, China would miss out on the economic and technological changes of the twentieth century. The country would fall further behind. Fortunately, soon after Mao's death in 1976, new leaders stepped up and China embarked on an exciting era of change and openness.

Mao's wife Jiang had wanted to succeed him as China's leader, but her unpopularity made that impossible. In October 1976, just weeks after her husband's death, Jiang and her close allies in Gang of Four were arrested. It took four years for the Gang of Four to be put on trial for crimes including treason. At her public trial in 1980, Jiang was defiant. She shouted to the judge, "Long live the Revolution!"[3] Sentenced to death, her term was changed to life in prison in 1983. According to many reports, she committed suicide in prison in 1991.

In June 1981, the Chinese Communist Party rendered judgment on Mao at the Eleventh Party Congress. They praised him for unifying a country broken by civil war and for establishing the People's Republic of China. But for the first time, the party criticized Mao for his mistakes and condemned the Great Leap Forward and the Cultural Revolution. His cult of personality was also considered with disapproval. Finally, China was ready to move forward.

# Deng Xiaoping

Before Mao died, he had allowed his close ally Deng Xiaoping to come back from exile. Like many Communist leaders, Deng was pushed from power during the Cultural Revolution. He had to apologize and write a self-criticism before he could return to power. A popular moderate, Deng took China's rudder in 1978. Although he did not hold an official top position, Deng was considered the leader of China until he retired in 1992.

Deng focused on modernizing the economy and opening China to the world. He introduced a market economy, which allows free competition, with prices set by supply and demand. Market economies stand in sharp contrast with Communism, which calls for production and wealth to be held by the state. Deng believed that a market economy could exist in a Communist nation.

To make the changes, Deng's government abolished the communes. People were allowed to start businesses and hire workers. Foreign investors imported raw materials and goods into special economic zones. Young Chinese went abroad to study science and technology. China was on its way to becoming one of the fastest-growing economies in the world. At the same time, Deng cracked down on protest and criticism. While he did not share all of Mao's strong views, Deng still maintained the strict authority of the Communist Party.

Some people felt the reforms did not go far enough. Others felt the changes went too far. Between April and June 1989, thousands of students, intellectuals, and others gathered in Beijing's Tiananmen Square to protest for more democratic reforms. The People's Liberation Army cracked down, opening fire on June 4. As many as 2,600 civilians were killed, and seven to ten thousand people were injured, sparking worldwide outrage.

## The Future

By 2015 China's population had grown to upwards of 1.4 billion people. Life expectancy had risen from about forty

In January 1979, Deng Xiaoping paid a formal visit to the United States. This was the first visit to the United States by a Chinese leader since the founding of the People's Republic of China. US President Jimmy Carter and Deng are shown speaking at a press conference.

years in 1950 to almost seventy years. China's large economy draws investors from around the globe. One the biggest exporters of goods, China also invests heavily in other countries in Africa, the Middle East, the United States, and elsewhere. Its entrepreneurs have become millionaires and billionaires. Chinese citizens are employed by multinational and Chinese companies that churn out computers, furniture, clothes, toys, and any consumer product that can find a market. Across China, new highways, roads, and bridges connect distant regions with booming cities. The world's longest high-speed rail system travels to new megacities rising up on farmland, ancient villages, and old city neighborhoods. Across China, sparkling modern high-rises reach for the sky. On the crowded streets of Beijing and

Shanghai, international businesspeople hurry to meetings to make deals, and young Chinese carry cell phones, tap into the Internet, and listen to music on earphones.

Such rapid changes in a society have led to challenges. China is the biggest emitter of carbon dioxide, the greenhouse gas that causes global warming. Air and water pollution caused by industries and coal-fired power plants create serious health problems for Chinese citizens and contribute to environmental problems worldwide. Beijing's sky is often hidden in a veil of smog. The fabric of China's society is also changing. The shift from a rural to industrial economy required millions of people to leave ancestral villages and farms to work in and around cities. Young people live far away from parents and grandparents.

## Human Rights

The fast pace of economic change has not been matched by advancements in freedom of expression or human rights. China's Internet, for example, is closely monitored. Nearly 650 million Chinese were online in 2015, but they were mostly blocked from communicating on Western social media sites. "A vast system of online censorship, commonly known as the Great Firewall, blocks the populace from viewing material deemed dangerous to the state," wrote Hanna Beech in *Time* magazine.[4] The government has tried to silence artists, writers, and political activists who criticize the Communist system. Civil rights activists and bloggers have been imprisoned. In 2010 Chinese dissident Liu Xiaobo, who took part in Tiananmen Square protests, won a Nobel Peace Prize, but could not travel to Norway to collect it. He was in a political prisoner in a Chinese prison.

**Chinese President Xi Jinping and US President Barack Obama speak during Obama's 2014 visit to China.**

The son of a Communist Party leader, Xi Jinping, was elected president by the National People's Congress in 2013. In his first speech to the congress, Xi urged the Chinese people to "bear in mind the mission, unite as one, and gather into an invincible force of wisdom and power." He went on, "All Chinese people deserve equal opportunities to enjoy a prosperous life, see their dreams come true and benefit together from the country's development." Xi looked ahead but revived some of Mao's values. Like Mao had done long ago, he called for a fostering of the "Chinese spirit," according to a report in *China Daily* newspaper.[5]

## Mao Is Remembered

Decades after his death, Mao casts a large shadow. His life was complicated and holds contradictions. "The scale of his life was too grand to be reduced to a single meaning," wrote

# Primary Source:
# A New Chinese Leader
# Looks to the Future

Throughout five thousand years and more of evolution as a civilization, the Chinese nation has made indelible contribution to the progress of human civilization. In modern times, however, China endured untold hardships and sufferings, and its very survival hung in the balance. Countless Chinese patriots rose up one after another and fought for the renewal of the Chinese nation, but all ended in failure. Since its founding, the Communist Party of China has made great sacrifices and forged ahead against all odds. It has rallied and led the Chinese people in transforming the poor and backward old China into an increasingly prosperous and powerful new China, thus opening a completely new horizon for the great renewal of the Chinese nation. Our responsibility now is to rally and lead the entire Party and the people of all ethnic groups in China in taking over the relay baton passed on to us by history, and in making continued efforts to achieve the great renewal of the Chinese nation, make the Chinese nation stand rock-firm in the family of nations, and make [an] even greater contribution to mankind.

*—Xi Jinping, the general secretary of the Central Committee of the Communist Party of China and later China's president, spoke about China's future at a press conference at the Great Hall of the People in Beijing on November 15, 2012.[6]*

biographer Alexander V. Pantsov.[7] He was poet, a statesman, a soldier, and a philosopher. He was a deep thinker and a teacher who studied literature, political philosophy, and Chinese history. A fearless soldier, Mao led men into battle and won a civil war. He was also a cruel and harsh leader.

Mao had big ideas, and didn't let anything  stand in his way. As Mao expert Jonathan D. Spence wrote, ". . . He possessed a relentless energy and a ruthless self-confidence that led him to become one of the world's most powerful rulers."[8] He ruled China with an iron fist, which fell on anyone who dared to disagree. Yet he also wanted China to succeed, and he was both a visionary and a realist, Spence observed. Mao knew the country needed to make changes in order to prosper in a changing world. Through revolution, Mao founded an independent China and began its industrialization. Mao's Communist Party promoted gender equality. Women held positions of power alongside men.

A diplomat who opened China to the West, Mao was also a brutal dictator, with little care for individual lives or human rights. As China's leader, he was responsible for the disastrous Great Leap Forward and the Cultural Revolution that resulted in the deaths of tens of millions of Chinese.

Nevertheless, the Chinese Communist Party protects Mao's image, despite acknowledging that he made mistakes. Open criticism of Mao is not allowed, and school children are taught a mostly positive view of Mao. "We must not abandon Marxism-Leninism and Mao Zedong Thought; otherwise, we will lose our foundation," Chinese President Xi said in 2012.[9]

As the twenty-first century unfolds, Mao's *The Little Red Book* is still being reprinted. In the book, Mao is quoted as saying: "The world is yours, as well as ours, but in the last analysis, it is yours. You young people, full of vigor and vitality, are in the bloom of life, like the sun at eight or nine in the morning. Our hope is placed on you. The world belongs to you. China's future belongs to you."[10] In a world that Mao could scarcely have imagined, Chinese young people are looking to the future with anticipation and hope.

# TIMELINE

1894–1895—War with Japan forces the Chinese to recognize Japan's control over Korea; China gives Japan the island of Taiwan.

1899–1901—During the Boxer Rebellion, peasant protests against Christian missionaries in China turn violent.

1911–1912—Chinese Revolution topples the Qing dynasty and establishes a republic; Sun Yat-sen founds provisional government in Nanjing.

1919—During the May Fourth Movement, students in Beijing protest the World War I peace treaty on May 4.

1921—Chinese Communist Party is formed in Shanghai by Mao Zedong and others.

1923—Sun Yat-sen forms United Front between the Kuomintang and the Chinese Communist Party.

1925—Death of Sun Yat-sen; Chiang Kai-shek becomes commander in chief of Kuomintang.

1927—Chiang Kai-shek takes over the Kuomintang and moves China's capital to Nanjing; Chiang starts the "White Terror" and purges Communists; Mao flees.

1928—The Kuomintang capture Beijing and unite China under one government.

1930—Mao establishes Communist base in the southern province of Jiangxi.

1931—Japan seizes China's northeast provinces.

1933—Chinese Communist Party grows to three hundred thousand members.

1934–1935—The Red Army undertakes the Long March to avoid an attack by the Nationalist Army; Mao leads the way.

1937—Japan invades China; The Communists and the Kuomintang join in the United Front to fight Japan.

1945—World War II ends with Japan's defeat.

# Timeline

1946—Truce between the Kuomintang and the Communists is
broken; Civil war resumes.

1949—Communists defeat the Kuomintang; On October 1, Mao
announces birth of the People's Republic of China.

1950—Chinese Communist troops join North Korean
Communists fighting the civil war in Korea.

1953—China's first Five-Year Plan starts; Korean War ends.

1957—Thousands of intellectuals criticize the government
during the Hundred Flowers Movement; Anti-Rightist
Campaign ends it in June.

1958—The Great Leap Forward is announced, setting new
production goals and creating People's Communes.

1960–1961—Massive famines sweep China after disruption in
agriculture; millions die.

1966—Mao launches the Cultural Revolution; *The Little Red
Book* is published by Lin Biao; formation of Red
Guards; chaos overtakes China.

1972—US president Richard Nixon meets with Mao in Beijing.

1976—Zhou Enlai dies; Deng Xiaoping is dismissed from his
posts; Mao dies on September 9.

1978—Deng Xiaoping becomes China's leader.

1980—Gang of Four is tried and sentenced.

1989—Troops fire on demonstrators protesting human rights
in Tiananmen Square; the official death toll is two
hundred. International outrage leads to sanctions
against China.

2010—Chinese dissident Liu Xiaobo, who took part in
Tiananmen Square protests, wins Nobel Peace Prize.

2012—Xi Jinping becomes chief of the Communist Party.

2013—Xi Jinping is made president; China quietly celebrates
the 120th birthday of Mao Zedong.

# CHAPTER NOTES

CHAPTER 1.   **The Long March**

1. Harrison E. Salisbury, *The Long March: The Untold Story* (New York: Harper and Row, 1985), p. 237.
2. Mao Tse-Tung, "On Tactics Against Japanese Imperialism," *Selected Works of Mao Tse-tung*, vol. I (Peking: Foreign Languages Press), https://www.marxists.org/reference/archive/mao/selected-works/volume-1/mswv1_11.htm (accessed August 2015).

CHAPTER 2.   **Son of a Rice Farmer**

1. Edgar Snow, *Red Star Over China* (New York: Grove Press, 1968), p. 132.
2. Ibid., p. 131.
3. Patricia Buckley Ebrey, *The Cambridge Illustrated History of China* (Cambridge: Cambridge University Press, 1997, p. 248.
4. Snow, p. 135.
5. Harrison E. Salisbury, *The Long March: The Untold Story* (New York: Harper & Row, 1985), p. 22.

CHAPTER 3.   **Uprising**

1. Edgar Snow, *Red Star Over China* (New York: Grove Press, 1968), p. 142.
2. Ibid., p. 146.
3. Alexander V. Pantsov, Steven I. Levine, *Mao: The Real Story* (New York: Simon & Schuster, 2013), p. 75.
4. Snow, p. 155.
5. Karl Marx and Friederich Engles, *The Communist Manifesto* (London, England: Verso, 2012), p. 34.
6. David Remnick, *Lenin's Tomb: The Last Days of the Soviet Empire* (New York: Random House, 2014), p. 506.

## CHAPTER 4.　**The Red Army**

1. Jonathan Spence, *Mao Zedong* (New York: Penguin, 2006), p. 75.
2. Mao Tse-Tung, "Analysis of the Classes in Chinese Society," *Selected Works of Mao Tse-tung* (Peking: Foreign Languages Press), https://www.marxists.org/reference/archive/mao/selected-works/volume-1/mswv1_1.htm (accessed August 2015).
3. Edgar Snow, *Red Star Over China* (New York: Grove Press, 1968), p. 258.
4. Mao Zedong, "On Guerrilla Warfare," *Selected Works of Mao Tse-Tung*, vol. VI, (Peking: Foreign Languages Press), https://www.marxists.org/reference/archive/mao/works/1937/guerrilla-warfare/ch01.htm (accessed August 2015).
5. Mao Zedong, "Basic Tactics," *Selected Works of Mao Tse-Tung*, vol. VI (Peking: Foreign Languages Press), https://www.marxists.org/reference/archive/mao/selected-works/volume-6/mswv6_28.htm#ch1 (accessed August 2015).
6. Harrison E. Salisbury, *The Long March: The Untold Story* (New York: Harper & Row, 1985), p. 129.

## CHAPTER 5.　**A New Leader**

1. Edgar Snow, *Red Star Over China* (New York: Harper & Row, 1985), p. 198.
2. Mao Zedong, "The Long March," in *Asia For Educators*, Columbia University, http://afe.easia.columbia.edu/special/china_1900_mao_march.htm (accessed August 2015).
3. Mao Zedong, "On Practice," *Selected Works of Mao Tse-tung*, vol. I (Peking: Foreign Languages Press), https://www.marxists.org/reference/archive/mao/selected-works/volume-1/mswv1_16.htm (accessed August 2015).

4. Chiang Kai-shek, "China Cannot Be Conquered," in Patricia Buckley Ebrey, *Chinese Civilization: A Sourcebook* (New York: Free Press, 2009), p. 402.

## CHAPTER 6.   The People's Republic

1 Mao Tse-tung, "The Chinese People Have Stood Up," *Selected Works of Mao Tse-Tung*, vol V (Peking: Foreign Languages Press), https://www.marxists.org/reference/archive/mao/selected-works/volume-5/mswv5_01.htm (accessed August 2015).

2. Li Zhi Sui, *The Private Life of Chairman Mao* (New York: Random House, 1996), p. 52.

3. Jonathan Spence, *Mao Zedong* (New York, Penguin, 2006), p. 118.

4. Mao Tse-tung, "On the Draft Constitution of the People's Republic of China," *Selected Works of Mao Tse-tung*, vol. V (Peking: Foreign Languages Press), https://www.marxists.org/reference/archive/mao/selected-works/volume-5/mswv5_37.htm (accessed August 2015).

5. Mao Tse-tung, "On the Cooperative Transformation of Agriculture," Selected Works of Mao Tse-tung, vol. V (Peking: Foreign Languages Press), https://www.marxists.org/reference/archive/mao/selected-works/volume-5/mswv5_44.htm (accessed September 2015).

6. "Constitution of the People's Republic of China," The National People's Congress of the People's Republic of China. http://www.npc.gov.cn/englishnpc/Constitution/2007-11/15/content_1372963.htm.

7. Ibid.

8. Mao Zedong, Introduction note to "Women Have Gone to the Labour Front," *Quotations from Chairman Mao Tsetung* (Peking: Foreign Languages Press, 1967), p. 297.

## CHAPTER 7. Drought and Famine

1. Jonathan Spence, *Mao Zedong* (New York: Penguin, 2006), p. 131.
2. Ibid.
3. Rose Tang, "Revolution's Children: The Collapse of Ideology Leaves Generations Adrift in a Moral Vacuum," *Asiaweek*, September 24, 1999, http://www.cnn.com/ASIANOW/asiaweek/magazine/99/0924/cn_journeys.html.
4. Ibid.
5. Mao Tse-tung, "The Masses Can Do Anything," *Selected Works of Mao Tse-tung*, vol. VIII (Peking: Foreign Languages Press), https://www.marxists.org/reference/archive/mao/selected-works/volume-8/mswv8_16.htm (accessed August 2015).
6. Ross Terrill, *China in Our Time* (New York: Simon and Schuster, 1992), p. 33.

## CHAPTER 8. "The East Is Red"

1. Alexander Pantsov and Steven I. Levine, *Mao: The Real Story* (New York: Simon and Schuster, 2012), p. 509.
2. Philip Short, *Mao: A Life* (New York: Henry Holt, 1999), p. 541.
3. Liang Heng and Judith Shapiro, *Son of the Revolution* (New York: Vintage Books, 1984), p. 68.
4. Jung Chang, *Wild Swans: Three Daughters of China* (New York: Simon and Schuster, 1991), p. 304.
5. Short, p. 543.
6. Jonathan Spence, *Mao Zedong* (New York, Penguin, 1999), p. 164.
7. Nien Cheng, *Life and Death in Shanghai* (New York: Grove Press, 1986), p. 274.
8. "The National Flag, National Emblem, and National Anthem of China," http://www.chinatoday.com/general/china-flag-emblem-anthem.htm (accessed August 2015).

9. Hugh Sidey, "Excursions in Mao's China," *Time*, March 6, 1972, 17.
10. Li Rhi Sui, *The Private Life of Chairman Mao* (New York: Random House, 1996), p. 86.
11. Mao Tse-tung, *Selected Works of Mao Tse-tung*, vol. I, https://www.marxists.org/reference/archive/mao/selected-works/volume-1/mswv1_2.htm.
12. Anchee Min, *Red Azalea* (New York: Berkley Books, 1994), p. 17.
13. "Nixon's China Odyssey," *Time*, March 6, 1972, 14.
14. Chang, p. 292.
15. Ibid.

## CHAPTER 9. **Raising the Bamboo Curtain**

1. Richard Nixon, *The Memoirs of Richard Nixon* (New York: Simon & Schuster, 1978), p. 553.
2. "Nixon's China Game, The American Experience," *PBS*, 1999, http://www.pbs.org/wgbh/amex/china/peopleevents/pande01.html.
3. "Nixon's China Game."
4. Henry Kissinger, *Years of Renewal* (New York: Simon and Schuster, 1999), p. 142.
5. "Nixon's China Odyssey," *Time*, March 6, 1972, 16.
6. Reuters, "Mao Tse-Tung Dies in Peking at 82," *New York Times*, September 10, 1976, 1.
7. Anchee Min, *Red Azalea* (New York: Berkley Books, 1994), p. 327.

## CHAPTER 10. **China After Mao**

1. Verna Yu, "China Still Dealing with the Legacy of Mao Zedong, 120 Years after His Birth," *South China Morning Post*, December 21, 2013, http://www.scmp.com/news/china/article/1386953/china-still-dealing-legacy-mao-zedong-120-years-after-his-birth.

# Chapter Notes

2. Andrew G. Walder, *China Under Mao: A Revolution Derailed* (Cambridge, MA: Harvard University Press, 2015), p. 13.
3. S.G. Breslin, *Mao* (Oxford, England: Routledge, 2014), p. 172.
4. Hanna Beech, "The Other Side of the Great Firewall," *Time*, June 11, 2015, http://time.com/3917721/the-other-side-of-the-great-firewall/.
5. Zhao Vinan, "Chinese Dream is Xi's Vision," *China Daily*, March 18, 2013, http://usa.chinadaily.com.cn/china/2013-03/18/content_16315077.htm.
6. "Xi Jinping's Remarks to the Press," The 18th National Congress of the Communist Party of China, November 16, 2012, http://www.china.org.cn/china/18th_cpc_congress/2012-11/16/content_27130032.htm.
7. Alexander V. Pantsov and Steven I. Levine, *Mao: The Real Story* (New York: Simon & Schuster, 2013), p. 576.
8. Jonathan Spence, *Mao Zedong: A Life* (New York: Penguin Books, 2006), p. xi.
9. Dexter Roberts, "China Contemplates Mao's Legacy on His 120th Birthday," *Bloomberg Business*, December 26, 2013, http://www.bloomberg.com/bw/articles/2013-12-26/china-contemplates-maos-legacy-on-his-120th-birthday.
10. Mao Tse-Tung, *Quotations from Chairman Mao Tse-Tung* (Peking: Foreign Languages Press, 1972), p. 288.

# GLOSSARY

**bourgeoisie**—The capitalist or middle class that owns most of society's wealth and power.

**capitalism**—An economic system with private or corporate ownership of goods, private investment, and open competition in a free market.

**commune**—A large state-owned farm where thousands of people share tools, resources, and labor.

**Communism**—A political and economic system in which the government owns the land and production, and wealth is distributed according to people's abilities and needs.

**cooperative**—A system in which rural villages share land and farm products.

**dissent**—To hold or express opinions that differ from those held by officials or the majority.

**dissident**—A person who speaks out against the government.

**Great Leap Forward**—The rapid industrialization and transformation of China to a Communist state from 1958 to 1961 caused a massive famine.

**hierarchy**—A system in which people are placed in a series of levels based on importance.

**imperialism**—The rule by an emperor or empress.

**peasant**—A poor farmer who owns or rents a small piece of land for subsistence farming.

**People's Republic of China**—The East Asian Communist nation formed in 1949 by Mao is the world's most populous country.

**propaganda**—Biased information that is spread to promote a point of view or political goal.

**radical**—Advocating a complete change in society or politics.

**revolutionary**—A person who works for political or social change.

**warlords**—The regional leaders in China who used force to control their kingdoms.

# FURTHER READING

## Books

Hay, Jeff. *The Chinese Cultural Revolution.* San Diego: Greenhaven Press, 2012.

Li, Moying. *Snow Falling in Spring: Coming of Age in China During the Cultural Revolution.* New York: Square Fish, 2010.

Luh, Shu Shin. *The Economy of China.* Broomall, PA: Mason Crest, 2012.

Yu, Chun. *Little Green: A Memoir of Growing Up During the Chinese Cultural Revolution.* New York: Simon & Schuster/Paula Wiseman Books, 2015.

Zedong, Mao. *Quotations from Mao Zedong.* New York: CN Times Books, 2013.

## Websites

**Long March**
www.history.com/topics/long-march
*An overview of the Long March by the History Channel.*

**Historic Figures: Mao Zedong**
www.bbc.co.uk/history/historic_figures/mao_zedong.shtml
*A look at Mao Zedong's life and achievements by the BBC.*

**Facts About Mao Zedong**
100leaders.org/mao-zedong
Time *magazine's biography of Mao Zedong.*

**Mao Zedong: Major Events**
www.columbia.edu/cu/weai/exeas/asian-revolutions/
leaders-mao-zedong.html
*A timeline of Mao's life.*

**Mao's Quotes**
www.morningsun.org/living/redbook/toc.html
*Quotations from Mao Zedong on a variety of topics.*

# INDEX

# Index

## H
Han Fei, 12-13
Hitler, Adolf, 54
Hong Kong, 17, 21
Hundred Flowers Movement, 76

## J
Japan, 9, 14, 17–18, 22, 24–25,
    27, 33, 46, 52–55, 57, 62–63, 99
Jiang Qing (Madame Mao), 49,
    93–94, 102, 108
Jiangxi Soviet, 38
Joint Communique, 102

## K
Kissinger, Henry A., 101–102
Korean War, 62–64, 98
Khrushchev, Nikita, 79
Kuomintang (National People's
    Party), 5, 7, 24, 32–33, 35–36,
    38–39, 41, 43, 46–48, 52,
    56–57, 79

## L
legalism, 12–13, 16, 73
Lenin, Vladimir Ilich, 30–31, 51,
    67, 114
Li Dazhao, 27, 31
Li Zhisui, 60–61, 92, 115
Lin Biao, 51, 81, 83, 94, 103
Ling-Ling and Hsing-Hsing, 97,
    102–103
*Little Red Book, The*, 86, 91, 93,
    114–115
Liu Shaoqi, 93
Liu Xiaobo, 111
Long March, 5, 7, 9, 43, 45–46,
    48, 50, 52, 67–68, 92

## M
Mao Yichang (father), 11, 13–14,
    28
Mao Zedong
    birth, 10
    childhood, 10–14
    children, 28, 41, 43, 48–49, 64
    and class struggle, 51, 96
    cult of, 90–92, 108
    death, 105
    education, 12–14
    health, 102, 105
    legacy, 106, 108, 112, 114–115
    and Maoism, 49–52
    mother, 11, 13
    and thought reform, 73
    wives, 41, 43, 48–49, 93–94,
      101–102, 108
Mao Zemin (brother), 11, 52
Mao Zetan (brother), 11, 43, 48
Marshall, George C., 56
Marx, Karl, 28, 30–31, 51
Marxism, 28, 50–51, 76, 114
May Fourth Movement, 25,
    27–28
missionaries, 18, 72

## N
Nanchang Uprising, 36
nationalism, 22
National Party Congress, 67–68
National People's Congress, 68,
    77, 112
*New Hunan*, 27
Nixon, Richard M., 97–99,
    101–104

## O
Opium War, 16–17

127